Belton House

Lincolnshire

Adrian Tinniswood

THE NATIONAL TRUST

The complete country house

Belton has almost everything you could hope to find in an English country house. From the outside, it looks very much as it did when first built in the 1680s – a masterpiece of glowing Ancaster stone and deceptively simple proportions. Inside, Belton still retains many of its original plasterwork ceilings and decorative wood carvings, but over the centuries it has been further enriched with collections that are now of national importance. Oriental porcelain complements the hand-painted Chinese wallpaper that fills a bedroom. A late 17th-century Soho tapestry provides a western fantasy vision of the exotic East. The magnificent silver includes a wine cistern big enough to bath a baby in. Richly tooled folios tell of generations of avid readers and discriminating collectors.

The lockplates throughout the house are engraved with the heraldic Brownlow greyhound

Key figures

Richard Brownlow (1553–1638) founded the family fortunes. He used the profits from his lucrative legal career in London to buy land, including the Belton estate.

Young Sir John Brownlow (1659–97) built the house in 1684–8, but did not live long to enjoy it, being killed in a shooting accident.

John, Viscount Tyrconnel (1690–1754) was much mocked as an ambitious, self-important, but almost entirely unsuccessful politician. Yet he had a keen eye for beautiful things, collecting much of the fine china and furniture you see today at Belton.

The 3rd Earl (1844–1921) *and Countess Brownlow* (1844–1917) presided over Belton during its High Victorian heyday, when it was home to the circle of aristocrat aesthetes known as 'the Souls'.

Perry, 6th Lord Brownlow (1899–1978) was briefly in the public spotlight as a close aide to Edward VIII during the 1936 Abdication Crisis.

The house is only the start. It sits within gardens both formal and informal. Avenues stretch into the distance, across the well-wooded park towards eye-catchers like the recently restored Belmount Tower.

The surrounding agricultural estate combined the pretty with the practical, in good times providing the income to keep the whole enterprise afloat.

For 300 years, Belton was the home of the Brownlows and then the Custs, who became powerful local landowners and, occasionally, figures of national significance. Their presence is still deeply felt throughout the house, in the family portraits that line the walls, and in their coats of arms, which appear on floors and ceilings, door handles and dinner plates. They may not always have been able to produce sons to inherit, but there was usually a nephew prepared to shoulder the responsibility of continuing the family line. And when death came, they were remembered in marble in the nearby church of SS Peter and Paul.

Supporting the family and the place through the centuries was an army of servants. They can be glimpsed sometimes in the Belton paintings. The porter Henry Jewell is shown standing proudly with his staff of office in front of the house. A black page boy wheels the invalid Lady Tyrconnel through the park. And when the house was threatened by rioters in 1831, the servants loyally rallied round to defend it.

The south front

Tour of the House

The Marble Hall

This is the principal room on the south side of the house. It is the grand opening to a formal procession of rooms, of which the Saloon, in the corresponding position on the north side, is the second stage.

The black and white squared *floor* (from which the room takes its name), and the arrangement of doors, windows and fireplaces, are original, while the panelling and carvings were substantially rearranged, and new doors were installed by Sir Jeffry Wyatville in the early 19th century. Two of the doors are false, being inserted purely for the sake of symmetry.

Decoration

Wyatville grained the panelling to imitate oak. In 1856 the room was repainted and revarnished. In 1980 Shirlie, Lady Brownlow painted it magnolia and white. Graining has been reintroduced in the manner of the Wyatville scheme.

Bringing limewood to life

The carving over the left-hand fireplace, with its game birds, peapods and ears of corn, may be the work of Grinling Gibbons, the supreme master of the technique in Britain. That over the right-hand fireplace is by Edmund Carpenter, who was paid £26 10s for the work in 1688. They were not conceived as a pair, and were probably moved here from other parts of the house in the late 19th century.

The Belton carvings were made from planks of limewood, a soft but very strong material perfectly suited to fine carving. Using a wide range of curved gouges, Gibbons mimicked the forms of nature with an illusionism and three-dimensional complexity unequalled until the era of computer-aided design.

Lying in state

The 1st Earl Brownlow died on 15 September 1853. As befitted a deeply traditional aristocrat, he was given an old-fashioned send-off. His body lay in state for three days in the Marble Hall, which was completely swathed in black for the occasion. His earl's coronet sat on the scarlet velvet coffin, surrounded by stands of black ostrich feathers (flowers were then reserved for the funerals of children or virgins).

Plasterwork

The *cornice and central ceiling rose* of 1811 are by Francis Bernasconi, who was often employed by Wyatville.

Pictures

Within the carvings over the fireplaces hang portraits of **Old Sir John Brownlow** (1594–1679) and his wife **Alice** (1604–76). They were a childless but devoted couple (their monument in Belton church shows them holding hands), and so bequeathed the estate to their great-nephew, **Young Sir John Brownlow** (1659–97), whose portrait hangs right of the entrance door.

The full-length portrait on the right-hand wall is of **Sir John Cust** (1718–70), who was painted by his friend Sir Joshua Reynolds in 1767–8 in his robes as Speaker of the House of

Commons. He is shown holding the first Bill he presented to George III. Sir John was given Belton by his mother to ensure his financial independence of government, but his health suffered from the stress of the turbulent politics of the day. On the north wall in the left-hand corner is his son *Sir Brownlow Cust* (1744–1807), who was given the peerage intended for Sir John before his premature death.

Flanking the door to the Saloon are Reynolds's portraits of *Sir Abraham Hume* (1749–1838) and his wife *Amelia* (1751–1809), who were both talented artists. Sir Abraham collected precious stones and Old Master paintings, some of which came to Belton after their daughter Sophia married Sir Brownlow Cust's son in 1810. Through Amelia, the great Ashridge estate passed to the family (see p. 58).

Sculpture

The *marble busts* portray three early 19th-century Prime Ministers and a king – from left to right, Spencer Perceval, the Duke of

Wellington, William IV and William Pitt the Younger.

Furniture

A pair of Regency 'Kent Revival' *side-tables* is supported by gilt crouching *greyhounds*, the first of many manifestations of the Brownlow crest at Belton, ranging from the engraved *lockplates* of the doors to the weathercock on the cupola. The mahogany *wheelback chairs* are dated by the arms on the backs to between 1770 and 1772, the period of the 1st Baron Brownlow's brief marriage to Jocosa Drury.

Ceramics

Five Kangxi blue-and-white porcelain *vases* stand on the tables. The smaller pair has unusual copper-red underglaze decoration.

On the left-hand mantelpiece are two beaker vases, two quatrefoil baluster vases, two Japanese saucers and a double gourd vase; on the right-hand one are two beaker vases, two Japanese vases, two foliate bowls and an egg-shaped vase.

The Saloon

This magnificent state reception room is placed on the main axis of the formal garden to the north. Until the 1770s it was known as the Great Parlour, the second in the procession of rooms from the Marble Hall. Although altered early in the 19th century, it retains much of its 17th-century atmosphere: the coloured marble fireplaces are original, and the ceiling is a successful Victorian pastiche in the style of the Caroline decorative plasterer Edward Goudge.

Decoration

It seems that the panelling was always varnished. During the Wyatville period it may have been partly gilded. It was altered in 1869.

Wood carvings

Edmund Carpenter's bill of March 1688, for £18, mentions work on an overmantel which corresponds to that at the east (right-hand) end of the room. The bolder and richer composition in the overmantel at the west (left-hand) end may be the work of Grinling Gibbons.

The drops of tumbling putti between the full-length pictures are the 19th-century work of W.G. Rogers, an authority on Gibbons who made similar carvings for Burghley House in Northamptonshire and Chatsworth in Derbyshire. The garlands over the doors could also date from this time.

Ceiling

The original plaster ceiling was replaced by Francis Bernasconi in 1811–12. Bernasconi's geometrically patterned ceiling fell down in 1877, and was itself replaced by George Jackson & Sons, who charged £258 7s in 1892. The design of garlands of fruit and flowers includes the arms of the 3rd Earl.

Pictures

The four full-length portraits flanking the door from the Marble Hall have hung here since at least 1688. To the right are *Young Sir John*

Brownlow (1659–97), the builder of the house, and his wife (and second cousin), *Alice* (1659–1721), who spent her long widowhood arranging grand marriages for their daughters. To the left are Young Sir John's younger brother, *Sir William Brownlow* (1665–1702), and his first wife, *Dorothy* (1667–99/1700), who was described as 'really deserving everybody's love'. Sir William inherited Belton from his brother in 1697, but allowed the widowed Alice to continue living here. The heads in all four portraits were probably painted by John Riley, the drapery by his assistant John Closterman – a common practice at the time.

Furniture

Pair of giltwood *pier-glasses and matching tables* decorated with Tyrconnel arms, *c*.1740. They support alabaster and Sicilian jasper slabs. Two Regency marble-topped *console tables* supported by carved and gilt eagles.

The Aubusson carpet was commissioned by the 1st Earl Brownlow on a trip to Paris in 1839

Two sets of carved walnut *armchairs*, *c*.1680, with cherubs on the legs and uprights as well as on the back rails and front stretchers. They were gilded in the 19th century.

Sculpture

Over the door from the Marble Hall is a Carrara marble bust of the young *Augustus Caesar*.

Ceramics

Two ormolu-mounted *gros bleu* Sèvres *vases mounted as lamps*, *c*.1774–93. The other vases and the chimneypiece decoration are all Japanese Imari, late 17th-century. The bottle-shaped vases were probably intended for sprinkling rose-water.

Carpet

The Aubusson carpet was commissioned by the 1st Earl, who visited the Aubusson factory on a trip to Paris in 1839. The Earl also ordered three pieces of carpet to fill the window embrasures.

Metalwork

The late 17th-century silver gilt *wall-lights* flanking the fireplaces bear the royal monogram 'WMR' for William and Mary, and were lent to Edward VIII during his brief period as king.

The Tyrconnel Room

In the late 17th century, this room was known first as the 'Drawing Room next to the greate Parlour', and then as the 'Green Damask Drawing Room'. By 1737 Viscount Tyrconnel had furnished it as a bedroom (the Crimson Room), when it was probably dominated by the huge bed now in the Blue Bedroom. Wyatville converted it into a Billiard Room in 1813, and this it remained until the 3rd Earl's late 19th-century remodelling.

Decoration

The room apparently retained its 18th-century decoration until the late 19th century, when it was panelled in oak with insets of crimson and white damask. The scrolled and gilded pelmets date from the period of Wyatville's work. The panelling seems to have been reused and has a similar look to that in the Saloon, which was altered in 1869. The damask in the panels is machine-made and so must date from the same period.

Carvings

The carving around the overmantel is probably a 19th-century pastiche by either George Jackson & Sons or W.G. Rogers, and was probably gilded when first put up. The carved frieze panel with Sir John Brownlow's monogram may be that referred to in Edmund Carpenter's bill of March 1688 as 'on frees for the same chimny with yr cipher'.

Pictures

Over the fireplace is another portrait of *Alice, Lady Brownlow* the wife of the builder of Belton, painted in the late 1680s by Godfrey Kneller. This formidable woman ruled Belton during her long widowhood, instilling terror in her daughters: on one occasion, they were so afraid that she would discover an illicit tea-party that they threw the teacups out of the window. Dame Alice's youngest daughter Eleanor was married to her cousin, *Sir John Brownlow, later Viscount Tyrconnel* (1690–1754), who is portrayed here full-length in his robes as a Knight of the Order of the Bath. The Chapel of Henry VII in Westminster Abbey, which was fitted up for the order in 1725, appears in the background. After Eleanor's death in 1730, Tyrconnel married *Elizabeth Cartwright* (d. 1780), whose portrait hangs on the far wall.

On the same wall is Tyrconnel's aunt, *Anne, Countess of Macclesfield* (1667/8–1753), who was at the centre of a famous 18th-century scandal. After falling out with her husband, she had two children by Richard Savage, 4th Earl Rivers, attempting to conceal the fact by wearing a mask during their delivery. Her husband found out and took her to court for adultery. The poet Richard Savage later claimed to be one of these children, although Anne maintained that both had died young. Tyrconnel also repudiated Savage, which led to a falling-out with his friend, the poet Alexander Pope.

Furniture

Queen Anne *pier-glass* – the pair to that in the Chapel Drawing Room. The arms of Young Sir John Brownlow and his wife appear in cut glass just below the cresting. The gilt frame is a later addition. Pair of *side-tables*, George II in style,

Floor

The unusual painted floor incorporates the Belton greyhounds and the Brownlow arms. Its date is uncertain; the form of the floorboards suggests a date in the 19th century.

with satyrs and paw feet, early 18th-century. The walnut *side-chairs* are a mixed early 18th-century set. On the floor under the table is a rare Charles II burr-walnut domed *coffer* with repoussé gilt-metal mounts and handles.

Clock

Early 18th-century ebonised *longcase clock* by the London clockmaker Daniel Delander (active 1699–1733).

Ceramics

A pair of Chinese Wucai ('five colours') *baluster vases*, mid-17th-century. The *blue-and-white china on the mantelpiece* includes a rare late Ming incense burner in the form of a fabulous lion, *c*.1680.

The Chapel Drawing Room

In the early 18th century this was known as the Blue Drawing Room, where Lord Tyrconnel displayed part of his porcelain collection and took tea, while his guests toured the garden: from the window you get a fine view of his Belmount Tower.

Decoration

This is one of the best surviving 17th-century interiors at Belton. The panelling was originally painted a brilliant blue flecked with gold, which has faded to green, thanks to the varnish applied by the house painter John Sparrow in 1772.

The late 17th-century *fireplace* was moved here from the Queen's Bedroom in 1859.

Pictures

Above the fireplace is *Richard Brownlow* (1553–1638) in his robes as Chief Prothonotary of the Common Pleas. His income from this lucrative post established the family's fortunes and enabled him to buy the Belton estate. Over the door to the Chapel Corridor is *Eleanor Brownlow* (1691–1730), youngest and prettiest daughter of Young Sir John Brownlow. Her marriage in 1712 to her cousin Sir John Brownlow, later Viscount Tyrconnel, kept Belton in the family.

Exotic encounters

The two *tapestries* are a 17th-century western vision of the exotic East. Combining Chinese, Indian and Turkish elements, they feature hunting scenes, fantastic amphibians, deities and noblemen and ladies with their entourages, all inhabiting a series of little islands in a snuff-coloured ocean. John Vanderbank (d. 1727), Chief Arras Worker of the Great Wardrobe, supplied them to Young Sir John Brownlow under the terms of an agreement dated August 1691, which stipulated that they should be of the same pattern as those which Vanderbank had created for Queen Mary's withdrawing room at Kensington Palace in the previous year.

Furniture

Cabinet on stand from Antwerp, late 17th-century. Queen Anne *pier-glass*, pair to the one in the Tyrconnel Room. English black *japanned side-table*, early 18th-century.
Three late 17th-century beechwood and walnut *armchairs*, two of which retain their original crimson silk velvet upholstery. Louis XIV Boulle *writing-table*, of the type known as a *bureau Mazarin*.

Ceramics

The porcelain is Japanese Imari.

9

The Chapel Gallery

The Chapel and its Gallery are among the interiors most representative of 17th-century Belton. The Gallery follows an arrangement common from the end of the Middle Ages, whereby the family 'closet', perhaps the most private of all the rooms in the house, opened on to the chapel at first-floor level.

The tablet in the doorway commemorates the restoration of Belton carried out in the 1960s by the 6th Lord Brownlow and his second wife, Dorothy.

Wood carvings

The panelling sets off what is possibly the finest of all the decorative carvings at Belton, with some of the peapods, wheat ears, fruit and flowers worthy of Grinling Gibbons himself.

Organ

An important work by the celebrated organ builder Thomas Elliott, installed in 1826. The profile medallion is of G.F. Handel. Hydraulic bellows, added in 1896, were driven by water power from the pump in the Wilderness.

Picture

The *Madonna and Child* is in the style of the Flemish artist Joos van Cleve (active 1511–40). The sleep of the Christ Child prefigures his death, and the grapes the wine drunk at Holy Communion.

Furniture

Two of the set of beechwood and walnut *chairs* from the Chapel Drawing Room, late 17th-century.

Ceiling

The Chapel and Gallery ceilings are both the work of Edward Goudge, who was paid in part for the work in 1687. The Gallery ceiling incorporates the arms of Brownlow at the east end and Sherard (Young Sir John's wife's family) at the west.

The Chapel

By the later 17th century the country-house chapel had become, in effect, a quasi-public room of state, like the great chamber and the best bedchamber. Young Sir John's Chapel reflects this trend: its opulence and splendour arise as much from the desire to express status as from more spiritual motives.

Decoration

The wooden reredos was painted to simulate marble in 1892, but it is not clear whether this was an entirely new scheme or the reinstatement of an earlier one. The panelling has been grained to imitate cedar since at least the mid-18th century.

Reredos

The reredos screen is perhaps the result of a collaboration between William Stanton, the mason-contractor in charge of the building of Belton, and a local carver such as Edmund Carpenter.

Carpenter may also have been responsible for the carvings surrounding the crimson silk velvet panel behind the altar; they are not of the same standard as those in the Gallery. The panel is signed 'Anne Cust fecert, 1769' and was put up to replace an earlier panel in 1771. The characteristic IHS (Jesus) monogram is embroidered in a sunburst, answering the quadrant rays at the corners.

Silver

On the altar is a 16th–17th-century Spanish *cross*, placed here to celebrate the coming-of-age of Viscount Alford in 1833.

The two pairs of silver *wall-lights* were originally made for the Crown and came to Belton around 1808 as the result of some sharp practice by the royal goldsmiths, Rundell, Bridge & Rundell. The King gave them to Rundells as bullion for a new commission, but this was made from other stock, and the sconces were then sold intact.

Return through the Chapel Drawing Room and enter the Staircase Hall via the door on the right.

The Staircase Hall

The placing of the main staircase off-centre is the only structural feature to break the overall symmetry at Belton. The Staircase Hall, known as the Little Marble Hall until about 1830, formed part of the ceremonial route for important visitors to the house, linking the Marble Hall with the Great Dining Room (now the Library) on the floor above. It retains its two finest 17th-century features: the paved floor by William Stanton and the plasterwork ceiling by Edward Goudge.

Staircase

The present staircase maintains Wyatville's decorative scheme, carried out in 1819. He retained the 17th-century walnut treads and risers, but replaced the original pear-wood balusters in oak.

The Wilton *carpet* was woven in 2001 following a pattern discovered on an early 19th-century carpet runner in the attics at Belton.

Decoration

The Vitruvian scroll (wave pattern) following the line of the stairs and the gold and white colours are Wyatville's and date from 1819. The wainscot was grained and the handrail varnished at the same period. The wainscot graining seems to have been painted out by the time Lord Brownlow had the room redecorated in the 1960s. It was restored in 2001.

Mythical beasts animate the legs of the Rococo giltwood stand

Plasterwork ceiling

This is by Edward Goudge, whose name appears in the account books in 1687. It incorporates the Brownlow crest of a greyhound in the corner cartouches, bordered by scrolling sunflowers and a garland of fruit and flowers.

Pictures

In the upper register are Godfrey Kneller's portraits of *Sir William Brownlow* (1665–1702) and his first wife *Dorothy* (1667–99/1700). Sir William was the younger brother of Young Sir John and father of Lord Tyrconnel.

Over the table below the stairs is *John, Viscount Alford* (1812–51), painted by Sir Francis Grant, the leading society portraitist of his day. Lord Alford died at 39 before he could inherit Belton, leaving his sons John and Adelbert to become 2nd and 3rd Earls Brownlow. The *3rd Earl Brownlow* (1844–1921) was painted around 1908 by Frank O. Salisbury, together with his wife, *Adelaide* (1844/5–1917) in the portraits hanging above the stairs.

The full-length hanging above the top flight depicts *Adelaide, Countess Brownlow* in a classical white dress 30 years earlier. Painted by Frederic Leighton in 1879, it is one of the masterpieces of Victorian art. The autumnal landscape in the background was inspired by the woodlands on the family's estate at Ashridge.

Sculpture

The marble bust of *George III* is by Richard Westmacott. The rare lead bust of the King's uncle, the *Duke of Cumberland*, by Henry Cheere was commissioned in 1746 by Lord Tyrconnel, who had loudly supported the Duke's brutal suppression of the Jacobite Rising at Culloden the previous year.

Furniture

Speaker Cust's leather-covered *robe chest*, on a contemporary mahogany stand. A late 17th-century or early 18th-century Japanese lacquer *coffer*, mounted on a Rococo giltwood stand with legs carved as mythical chimera, c.1740. Ormolu *chandelier*, 1830s, acquired from the Lansdowne House sale in 1931. Pair of 18th-century *starting cannon*.

The Blue Dressing Room

This little dressing room was opened to visitors for the first time in 2005 as a picture cabinet to house the remaining Old Master paintings from the collections of Lord Tyrconnel and the 1st Lord and the 1st Earl Brownlow. It has been redecorated to match the Blue Bedroom.

Pictures

They include the **Madonna and Child** attributed to the Florentine artist Fra Bartolommeo (1472–1517). The composition was strongly influenced by the tender Madonnas painted by Raphael during his years in Florence (1504–8). It came from the collection of Sir Abraham Hume, who bought it in Florence in 1787.

François Boucher (1703–70) painted *La vie champêtre* (*The Country Life*) early in his career, in a Dutch style quite different from the erotic and sentimental images with which he later made his name. It came here with Sir Henry Bankes's collection, but was sold by the 6th Lord Brownlow in 1929. It was later acquired by

The late 17th-century Italian cabinet in the Blue Dressing Room is decorated with panels of immensely expensive lapis lazuli

Dr Ernst Sklarz, whose widow bequeathed it to the National Trust so that it could be returned to Belton.

Furniture

The Lapis lazuli *cabinet* of architectural form is Italian, late 17th-century. The Charles II giltwood stand is thought not to be the original, which may now be supporting the lacquered coffer in the Red Drawing Room. The use of such a quantity of lapis lazuli, which is set in panels bordered with ebonised and parcel-gilt mouldings, is extremely rare; with its magnificent gilt stand carved with putti, acanthus branches and garlands of flowers, this is one of the most extravagant pieces of furniture at Belton. It was acquired at the 1984 Belton sale with support from the V&A purchase grant fund.

La vie champêtre; by François Boucher

The Blue Bedroom

In the late 17th century this room was occupied by Young Sir John's brother-in-law, Sir John Sherard, whose portrait by Riley hangs here. Sir John became so addicted to gambling on the dice-game Hazard that he had to lodge a £2,000 guarantee with his brother-in-law to stop himself from indulging.

Decoration

In 1778 James Wyatt submitted designs for the chimneypiece and for the cornice and frieze, which were installed about 1780 and are still in place. Recent redecoration of this room has relied on evidence from documentary and physical research. The block-printed distemper wallpaper, especially printed to a design of c.1830, resembles the paper that hung on the walls in the mid-19th century. The oak-grained dado conforms with this historical scheme. A detailed upholsterer's bill of 1813 enabled the re-creation of the silk damask and striped tabouret case covers for the seat furniture, which was designed to accompany the silk damask bed.

Pictures

Over the mantel hangs the portrait of *Sir John Sherard* (1662–1724) by John Riley. The other portrait is of *Sir Thomas Drury* of Overstone (1712-59) by Thomas Hudson.

Furniture

The *mantel clock* in a scarlet tortoiseshell case, c.1710, is by Thomas Vernon of London. English oyster-veneered laburnum-wood *domed coffer* on a stand, late 17th-century. A set of four walnut and beechwood *chairs* and an *armchair*, all late 17th-century. They are in the style of the royal furniture-maker Thomas Roberts.

The *bureau-cabinet*, veneered in burr walnut, c.1715, is one of the finest pieces in the house. The doors of the cabinet retain their original engraved mirror plates and open to reveal an elaborate interior with tiers of drawers and pilasters of *verre églomisé* (painted glass).

Ceramics

The mantelpiece decoration is formed from a selection of *blanc-de-Chine* figures and tea bowls. *Blanc-de-Chine* is oriental porcelain which is glazed pure white with no added colours.

Bed

The bed is in the style of Francis Lapiere, a French Catholic craftsman working in England in the early 18th century. It closely resembles a bed made around 1704–10 for Dyrham Park, near Bath, and may have been acquired by Dame Alice, widow of Young Sir John Brownlow. It may originally have had crimson or embroidered hangings (traces of crimson silk were found on the bed-frame during conservation work). First reupholstered in 1813, it was hung with blue silk damask, and at the same time the curtain pelmets, the curtains and some of the furniture were covered to match. At over 4.9 metres high, the bed is unusually tall for the period. As originally configured, it was a conventional four-poster. The conversion to the present 'angel tester' form may have coincided with the reupholstery of 1813. The bed-hangings were conserved in 2002. Earlier, in 1994, new silk damask bed curtains were woven to match. The window curtains were made up and the pelmets re-covered in 2005.

The Library

This room has twice been transformed since the 17th century, when it was the Great Dining Room. In 1778 James Wyatt changed it into a classical drawing room with a shallow vaulted ceiling in delicate plasterwork, and swept away all traces of its original Caroline decoration. In 1876 the 3rd Earl converted it into a library. The *doors* are fine examples of Neo-classical design and craftsmanship, made of Cuban mahogany.

In bouncing good health

The exercise chair or 'library horse' was an 18th-century precursor of the exercise bicycle. Bouncing up and down on it was thought to be good for the health. Sadly, it is unlikely to be that made for Lord Tyrconnel in 1754 (the year of his death) by his own joiner, Samuel Smith, who was paid £2 19s 2d 'for a new Chamber Horse which my Lord bespoke himself', as it would appear to date stylistically from 50 years later.

Decoration

Wyatt's plasterer may well have been the otherwise unknown Utterton, who was paid £67 7s for decorating the adjoining Boudoir (see p. 24) in 1777, and received a further £63 for unspecified work two years later.

Elizabeth and Lucy Cust painted the putti in the lunettes at either end of the room in the early 19th century. (Wyatt had proposed to fill them with mythological scenes, which were never commissioned.) The present decoration dates from the 1960s.

Chimneypiece

The marble chimneypiece has caryatids representing Ceres and Pomona (the Roman goddesses of the earth and of fruit) and a bacchic frieze. Attributed to Sir Richard Westmacott, RA, it was not part of Wyatt's scheme for the room, which had a more delicate chimneypiece with columns supporting an overmantel mirror extending the whole height of the wall.

Bookcases

These were designed for Sir Jeffry Wyatville, perhaps by his cousin Edward Wyatt, and made in 1809, originally for what are now the Hondecoeter and Breakfast Rooms (see p. 30). They were installed in the Library by the Grantham firm of John Hall in 1876. Originally pale oak with oak-grained panels to the cupboards, they were painted white in the 1960s.

Pictures

The portrait over the fireplace is of the *1st Earl Brownlow* (1779–1853), who commissioned the bookcases now here and bought many of the books they contain.

Furniture

English *desk*, *c.*1760. Several pieces of *library furniture* which correspond with early 19th-century designs from Gillow & Co. of Lancaster.

Speaker Cust's *despatch boxes* rest on contemporary mahogany stands. They were offered to Winston Churchill for use in Parliament, when the House of Commons was bombed in 1941.

Books

The library collections at Belton are among the finest in any National Trust house. The Library and Study each contain about 6,000 books. They give an almost complete picture of book-collecting over 350 years, starting with the collection of Richard Brownlow the Prothonotary. There are bookplates or signatures of over a hundred family members, including Young Sir John and Dame Alice Brownlow. There are a few 16th–18th-century manuscripts, but the majority of the books are printed, the oldest being a New Testament commentary printed in Nuremberg in 1493.

The greatest collectors were Viscount Tyrconnel, Speaker Cust and his son, the 1st Baron, and his son, the 1st Earl. The more impressive volumes, and the best bindings, are mostly in the Library, with the Study housing more workaday editions. A catalogue of Tyrconnel's books at his death in 1754 lists over 2,200 titles, most still on the shelves at Belton. They include important scientific works by Isaac Newton and others, in addition to history, travel, theology, literature and the classics – both older books and current publications, published in France, Holland and Italy as well as Britain. The Speaker and the 1st Baron also collected enthusiastically, adding politics to Tyrconnel's interests, and subscribed to many books as they were published. The 1st Earl travelled widely – even buying books in Russia – and had a special interest in archaeology and local history, and (like Tyrconnel) also in Italy: there is a fine collection of editions of Italian literature.

The Yellow Bedroom

This is one of James Wyatt's surviving late 18th-century interiors. Originally called the 'White Painted Room', Lord Tyrconnel refurnished it in green and white. By 1754 the abundance of needlework upholstery gave it an added femininity. Wyatt did away with the four side windows, and opened the view of the park to the south through the present window arrangement. The room became known as the Yellow Bedroom sometime after 1830.

Decoration

Wyatt's decoration dates from 1777–8. Drawings show details for the cornice frieze, which was to have been matched in the upper part of the door entablature. Wyatt also designed the overmantel mirror.

Bed

Regency mahogany four-poster bed with gilt-wood ornaments and cornice, with cream-coloured flossy silk couched work incorporating the monogram of Marian, Lady Alford, mother of the 2nd and 3rd Earls. The piece was made up into a bed in 1927.

Pictures

In the centre of the right-hand wall is a *View of Greenwich* painted by Robert Griffier in 1729, the year that Lord Tyrconnel took a house in Greenwich for the sake of his sick wife, Eleanor. Sadly, the change of air did not help: she died the following year. The view of Greenwich shows Wren's still uncompleted Royal Naval Hospital (now the University of Greenwich).

Flanking the Greenwich view are Sir Francis Grant's portraits of *Marian, Lady Alford* (1817–88), painted in 1841, the year of her marriage, and of her elder son, *John, 2nd Earl Brownlow* (1842–67), painted to celebrate his coming-of-age in 1863. He suffered from tuberculosis and died only four years later at Menton.

Furniture

Pair of Regency mahogany *bedside cupboards* with ormolu mounts. Pair of early 18th-century *side-chairs* and a mahogany *fire-screen*, all embroidered in 17th-century manner by, or after, Lady Marian Alford, a historian of needlework who wrote the book *Needlework as Art* and helped to found the Royal School of Needlework. Regency mahogany *sofa-table and chest-of-drawers* in the manner of Gillow & Co. Regency mahogany *wash-stand*. Giltwood *pier-glass*, mid-18th-century.

The Chinese Bedroom

The wallpaper is 18th-century, but was not put up here until about 1840. It is difficult to decide whether the room was fitted to the wallpaper or vice versa. The proportions of the room have been altered since the late 17th century, when it was known as 'the drawing roome next to the best Chamber': on the south side, a false wall has been erected, making a passage between the Queen's Bedroom and the East Landing. The cornice, dado and other joinery are painted to imitate bamboo.

Rare mirror black Sèvres porcelain on the mantelpiece in the Yellow Bedroom

The Chinese Bedroom

Chinamania

The *Chinese wallpaper* is decorated with a continuous scene of a garden party running around the lower part. The paper is made up of square, hand-painted sections and in places some of the birds and butterflies were cut out and applied separately.

Chinese wallpapers were first imported to Britain in the late 17th century and became fashionable, particularly as decoration for women's bedrooms. They were part of the craze for all things Chinese observed by James Cawthorne in his *Essay on Taste* (1756):

Of late 'tis true quite sick of Rome and Greece,
We fetch our models from the wise Chinese,
European artists are too cool and chaste,
For Mand'rin is the only man of taste.

Pictorial designs of this kind were produced purely for export. The Chinese preferred to paper their walls with plain patterns.

Bed

The bed, *c.*1840, has a gilded and scrolled canopy and glazed chintz hangings and matching curtains. The coverlet is early 19th-century red embroidered satin from Canton.

Furniture

This room houses some of the collection of *japanned wares* included in the original furnishing of Belton. Chinese lacquer *coffer* with engraved gilt-metal angles and lockplates, late 17th-century. Purchased at the Belton sale in 1984 with the help of generous benefactions.

Carpets

Aubusson carpet and hearth rug, 19th-century.

Ceramics

Above the fireplace are Chinese *famille verte* porcelain and a pair of Chinese *cloisonné* enamel *quails*, late 18th-century.

The Queen's Bedroom

This room takes its name from William IV's widow, Queen Adelaide, for whose visits in July 1840 and September 1841 it was redecorated. Prior to that, the room had changed its name at least four times and had been used both as a bedroom and as a picture room. Centrally situated over the Saloon, it was originally known as the 'Best Chamber'.

Decoration

The panelling, which dates from the building of the house, was stripped in the mid-20th century. It has been redecorated to resemble its appearance at the time of Queen Adelaide's residence in the house. The furnishing also dates from this early Victorian redecoration.

Chimneypiece

The marble chimneypiece is early Victorian.

Wood carving

The carved wood frieze panel above the fireplace may be one of those for which Edmund Carpenter was paid in 1688.

Bed

This is probably the canopy bed with a dome upholstered in 1813 by William Stephens, later refurbished in the revived Rococo style, with a parcel-gilt canopy and Queen Adelaide's monogram in silver embroidery on the headboard. The crimson and ivory striped silk used for the bed-hangings, curtains, chairs, sofa and pole-screens was rewoven in 1998 to match the original striped silk, which had decayed to an irreparable state. The braids, fringes and tassels, however, are all original and have been carefully cleaned and repaired before being reapplied to the bed and the curtains.

The bedhead is embroidered in silver thread with Queen Adelaide's monogram

Pictures

Alice Brownlow probably used this as her bedroom during her long widowhood in the early 18th century, which she spent arranging marriages for her daughters. Portraits of two of them hang here: over the fireplace is *Elizabeth* (1681–1723), who in 1699 married the 6th Earl of Exeter from nearby Burghley; next to her is *Alice* (1684–1727), who in 1703 married Francis, 2nd Lord Guilford.

Furniture

Pair of Regency mahogany *bedside cupboards* with ormolu mounts, which resemble published designs by Gillows. Dutch marquetry *armoire*, the panels of flowers attributed to the 17th-century master Van Maekeren.

Textiles

19th-century Aubusson *carpet*. Set into the panelling on either side of the room are two interesting *panels of linen*, printed to resemble tapestry, with flower baskets and vases among stringwork scrolls inhabited by birds.

Ceramics

On the bedside cabinets are early 18th-century Japanese Imari *vases mounted as lamps*.

A royal widow

Princess Adelaide of Saxe–Coburg and Meiningen married the future William IV in 1818. She was a natural peace-maker, and the marriage proved happy, despite the differences in their ages (she was 25, he 52), his ten illegitimate children (their children died in infancy), and the fact that they had not met before the marriage.

The 1st Earl's third wife, Emma, served as the Queen's sole lady-in-waiting at the Coronation in 1831: it was her job to attach the Queen's crown with four diamond hat-pins. Lady Brownlow became a friend, inviting Adelaide to Belton after the King's death in 1837.

Ceramics

The porcelain at Belton is a fine cross-section of what one would hope to find in a house of its size and date. It falls into three categories – late 17th- and very early 18th-century Japanese and Chinese wares, mid-18th-century English porcelain and Chinese *famille rose*, and late 18th-century and very early 19th-century Sèvres, Paris and Meissen porcelain. The first two categories are well represented in this room.

Much of the early porcelain is Japanese, painted in a basic palette of red, blue and gold, and commonly known as Imari after the port in southern Japan near where it was made. The most notable example is the large bowl on the lacquer cabinet in this room. The Imari wares mostly date from 1690–1720 and are intermingled with a number of almost indistinguishable Chinese copies made in 1710–30, for example the bowl in the recessed cabinet to the left of the door to the Library. Japanese export porcelain was popular in many European stately homes in the early 18th century, when some of the pieces here could have been acquired, but many came to the house from Cockayne Hatley, the 5th Lord Brownlow's family home in Bedfordshire, when he inherited Belton in 1921.

Among the fine Japanese pieces are a number of interesting shapes, such as the fan-shaped dishes in the free-standing cabinet. There are also two square vases of Kakiemon type shaped like Dutch gin bottles and painted with birds and flowering plants. The palette, which

The Ante-Library

Except for a short spell as a bedroom, until 1876 this was the dressing room to the adjoining Morris Room (not shown to the public), although being next to the best bedchamber (now the Queen's Bedroom), it may also have been used by the occupants of that room: it probably served as Queen Adelaide's dressing room during her visits in 1840 and 1841.

The 3rd Earl made it into an Ante-Library when the Library was fitted out in 1876 – the press-numbers survive around the tops of the cases – but more recently the room has been used as a china cabinet to display some of Belton's best porcelain.

Decoration

The *fireplace and overmantel* are probably original to the room. The marbling seems to date from 1884.

(Right) A late 17th-century Japanese Imari bowl

includes a brown, suggests that they were decorated at a rival kiln to the Kakiemons, c.1680.

Chinese *famille verte* of the late Kangxi period (c.1690–1722) is well represented here. It is interesting to contrast the *famille verte* colours with the Kakiemon enamels of the two dishes in the same cabinets. Of particular interest is a composite vase: a Chinese café-au-lait triple gourd bottle on a Japanese Arita jar, which itself stands on a Chinese blue-and-white ginger jar, all dating from the late 17th century. Assembling masses of china in this way was characteristic of the chinamania brought to Britain by Queen Mary at that period. The Ante-Library also contains a small collection of Chinese porcelain, mostly of the same date, made at Dehua in the southern province of Fujian, more commonly known in Europe as *blanc-de-Chine*.

Of the two blue-and-white part armorial services in the Ante-Library, one has the arms of Sir Richard Cust and his wife Anne Brownlow in *famille rose* enamels in the centre, c.1730, while the other of the same date has the arms of Viscount Tyrconnel at the top. Other armorial pieces show different connections: the dish with

Chinese Imari-style teapot

the arms of Cookson must have come with the marriage of Henry Cust of Cockayne Hatley to Sara, daughter of Isaac Cookson, while the tea caddy with the arms of Egerton entered the house with the marriage in 1810 of the future 1st Earl Brownlow to Sophia, granddaughter of John Egerton.

Of about the mid-1750s is a set of Chinese *famille rose* plates and dishes with silver pheasants within elaborate borders (Ante-Library and Red Drawing Room). In the same case in the Ante-Library as the blanc-de-Chine there are a very fine *famille rose écuelle* (bowl) and a pair of plates painted with irises in the style of the Dutch-German botanical artist Maria-Sybilla Merian.

Walk through the Library, which is described on p. 16, to reach the Boudoir.

A Chinese Kangxi period famille verte plate
(Right) A Chinese blanc-de-Chine white goddess

The Boudoir

This was originally furnished as a bedroom. In 1776–7 the room was entirely remodelled by James Wyatt as Lady Brownlow's dressing room in Neo-classical style. Some of Wyatt's design remains, in particular the ceiling and cornice frieze, but since then it has been used as both a sitting room and a bedroom. The 3rd Earl had the panels and large overmantel installed in the 1870s. The room was redecorated in 1963 as a boudoir.

Decoration

The plasterwork ceiling has been repainted as it was originally conceived. The plasterer may have been Utterton (see p. 16). Wyatt's elevations show the walls a plain colour, probably the 'Green Flock Palm Paper' bought in 1777. The 3rd Earl's panels were originally filled with green striped damask; these panels, together with the appliqué drops of acanthus husks, a new chimneypiece with paired columns at either side and the oval overmantel mirror, were produced by George Jackson & Sons. In the 1960s the chimneypiece was removed and the decayed damask replaced with flock-paper.

Chimneypiece

The chimneypiece was replaced in the 6th Lord Brownlow's time by one more in keeping with the room, with inset copper plaques in the manner of Angelica Kauffman, representing Juno, Minerva and Apollo. Though not included among Wyatt's surviving designs, this may be the original chimneypiece, which must have been the work of William Tyler (d. 1810), who had executed monuments in Belton church to Speaker Cust and his wife, and who is mentioned by Wyatt in an annotation on his drawing of a carpet design for this room.

Pictures

On the east wall are portraits of four of the daughters of Sir Richard and Anne Cust, who inherited Belton on the death of her brother, Lord Tyrconnel, in 1754: *Jane* (1725–91) and *Lucy* (1732–1804), both painted by Thomas Hudson in 1756; *Dorothy* (1729–70) and *Elizabeth* (1724–69).

On the west wall are pastel portraits by William Hoare of Bath of *Sir Henry Bankes* (1711–74) and his wife *Frances* (1728–1806). Their daughter Frances married the 1st Lord Brownlow and inherited their important picture collection, part of which is still at Belton.

Furniture

Fine late 18th-century marquetry and giltwood *pier-table* with an elliptical top. Mahogany *silver table* in the Chinese Chippendale style. Chinese lacquer *cabinet* with copper mounts on a mid-17th-century giltwood stand, with a 19th-century Regency ormolu gallery rail added on three sides. A large *overmantel mirror* in the style of Wyatt, made in 1875.

Carpet

Aubusson tapestry carpet, *c.* 1900. Although Wyatt offered two alternative designs for a carpet for this room, both of which mirrored the ceiling, there is no evidence that either was ever woven.

Figures of fun

The two uncoloured Bow *porcelain figures*, *c.* 1750–2, represent Henry Woodward and Kitty Clive, the greatest comic actors of their day, in costume as the 'Fine Gentleman' and the 'Fine Lady' in David Garrick's farce, *Lethe*, which was first produced in 1740. The play poked fun at the behaviour of theatre audiences and at such fashionable topics as marriages of convenience and landscape gardening.

The Windsor Bedroom

Named in honour of Belton's association with Edward VIII, although the present Prince of Wales, while a cadet at RAF Cranwell, was the most frequent visitor to use the room in recent times. It was last decorated for the 6th Lord Brownlow's third wife, Leila.

(Above) The Windsor Bedroom

Pictures

Either side of the windows are *Perry Brownlow* (1899–1978) and his first wife *Kitty* (d.1952). Over the mantelpiece is a painting of *Edward VIII arriving at Westminster* for his first (and only) state opening of Parliament in 1936, by Edward Halliday.

The mysterious *Profile of an unknown woman* in the style of John Singer Sargent has provoked more speculation than any other picture at Belton, but her identity still remains a secret.

Furniture

Late 18th-century giltwood and composition *cheval-fire-screen* with a tapestry banner.
Late 18th-century mahogany *serpentine dressing-chest and basin stand*.

Ceramics

A collection of Sèvres cups, saucers, plates and other European porcelain.

Edward VIII and the Brownlows

Perry, 6th Lord Brownlow was a trusted friend and adviser to Edward VIII during the Abdication Crisis of 1936. In December he accompanied Wallis Simpson when she left Britain for the South of France, where he tried unsuccessfully to persuade her to give up the King.

The Windsor Corridor

Picture and sculpture

The Library at Chancellor's House depicts Nina Cust sitting in the Custs' 17th-century house in Hyde Park Gate (now demolished). 'Nina's décor made it seem like a house in the country.' She was a talented sculptor, who modelled a *self-portrait bust*, a plaster copy of which is displayed in the niche over the door at the far end of the Windsor Landing.

The West Staircase

Known in the late 17th century simply as the 'Staircase by the Dining Room Door', this was originally used only by servants. It was probably altered by Wyatville *c.*1810, and acquired a new importance when the 1st Earl turned the West Entrance into the family entrance, and revived the habit of using the west side of the house as the family's living quarters.

Pictures

The huge anonymous *View of Belton, c.*1720, depicts the south front enclosed by a wrought-iron screen. The outsize figure of the porter Henry Jewell stands in front of the gates ready to greet the arriving coach and walk the guests to the front door. (The forecourt was too small to admit coaches, so it was later enlarged by Lord Tyrconnel.) Jewell's staff hangs beside the painting. He was buried in the churchyard.

At the bottom of the stairs hangs the equally large *Cust Family*, painted about 1741 by Enoch Seeman, who was chosen because he was cheaper than the first choice, William Hogarth. It depicts the widowed Anne Brownlow, Lady Cust, with her children (Anne also appears as a young woman in Kneller's 1719 portrait on the north wall of the stairs.) Sitting in the centre is her eldest son, Sir John Cust, to whom she passed Belton on inheriting it from her brother, Lord Tyrconnel. Sir John holds a miniature of his new wife, Etheldred Payne. The oval painting of a boy at the top right may commemorate a dead son.

Sculpture

The marble bust on the side-table is of *Henry Cust* (1861–1917), who had expected to inherit Belton from his much older and childless cousin, the 3rd Earl Brownlow, but, in the event, predeceased him. The bust was carved by his long-suffering wife Nina, who remained devoted to him despite his numerous infidelities.

Furniture

Two late 17th-century walnut and gilt *pier-glasses*. An incised lacquer *chest* of coromandel, a wood from the south-eastern coast of India.

The Ante-Room

In Lord Tyrconnel's day the Ante-Room was the 'Little Room by the Library'. The 1737 inventory shows that its contents included two chairs (one of which was a 'black leather

Nina Cust in her library at Chancellor's House in London. The safe painted with Adam-style motifs (in the left foreground) is now in the Study

(Above) The Study

bottomed chair on wheels'), 34 prints and a 'map of Belton'. Today, it is a sitting area for visitors, and contains framed maps of the estate and park and a mid-18th-century view of Belton from the park (over the mantelpiece).

The Study

In the late 17th century this was known as 'the School Room', presumably forming part of a suite of rooms for Young Sir John Brownlow's daughters, whose nurseries were directly above. By 1737 it was Viscount Tyrconnel's library, and it has remained essentially a male preserve ever since. Tyrconnel probably painted it a dull green colour similar to the present decoration.

Books

The books in the Study are rather less impressive to look at than those in the Library – though perhaps more used – but they include several fine bindings and some 18th-century music (both printed and manuscript), in addition to a wide range of literature, theology and history. There are sets of parliamentary debates and many books on law, from the early 16th to the 19th centuries – as well as early works on cookery and medicine. There are long runs of periodicals, ranging from the *Gentleman's Magazine*, starting in 1731, to the *Racing Calendar* for 1809–52. The floor-to-ceiling shelving gives a splendid impression of being totally surrounded by books, increased by the dummy bindings covering the gaps between shelves, lettered with joking titles such as *Paradise Improved* or *Law without Fees*, but the bronzed busts of men of letters and science, a feature of 18th-century libraries, were intended to inspire the reader to serious study.

Furniture

The green-painted iron *'safe' cabinet* came from Harry and Nina Cust's London house and can be seen in the painting on the Windsor Corridor (see p. 26).

The Tapestry Room

The room was remodelled *c.*1890 in convincing 17th-century style by the 3rd Earl Brownlow, who wanted a setting for the Diogenes tapestries. New panelling in oak was provided for the walls, and George Jackson & Sons put up the pastiche plaster ceiling. The same company probably also supplied the limewood carvings above the chimneypiece.

In the 17th century it had served as a dining room, and in the 18th century as a common parlour. The room was redecorated by Wyatville in 1811, but all that survives from the Wyatville period is the fireplace.

Pictures

Above the fireplace hangs a further portrait of Young Sir John's daughter *Eleanor* (1691–1730), who married Viscount Tyrconnel to keep the estate in the Brownlow family.

Furniture

Louis XV kingwood *commode*, stamped twice by the *maître ébéniste* François Mondon (1694–1770). Gilt gesso *pier glass*, *c.*1700. Early 18th-century giltwood *side-table* with cover of 18th-century silver-thread flowered brocade. Louis XIV scarlet *bureau Mazarin* with Boulle decoration (tortoiseshell and brass inlay).

The good life

The tapestries illustrate scenes from the life of the ancient Greek philosopher Diogenes, who believed that a simple, natural life was the way to happiness. They were inspired by the 17th-century Italian artist Salvator Rosa, and were probably made in the early 18th century at the Mortlake factory south-west of London. The borders, incorporating the arms of Viscount Tyrconnel, are of a slightly later date. They are said to have been found in the attics, being used as carpets.

Left of fireplace: *Alexander visiting Diogenes in his tub*; Right of fireplace: *The School of Plato*; Facing fireplace: *Diogenes writing on the lintel above the door of the cave*; Facing fireplace: *Diogenes breaking the cup*

Clock

Louis XV Boulle bracket clock. The case dates from *c.*1750, with a later movement by Vulliamy, *c.*1850.

Ceramics

An ormolu-mounted *famille verte* hexagonal bottle vase and a garniture of lobed hexagonal Kangxi blue-and-white vases.

(Left)
The Tapestry Room

(Right)
The Red Drawing Room

The Red Drawing Room

This has always been one of the most lavishly decorated and furnished rooms in the house. In 1698 it was described as the 'White Varnished Drawing Room' and was filled with expensive gilt and japanned furniture.

In 1811 the room was completely redecorated by Wyatville, and the furnishings were updated by the 1st Earl in the 1830s. The recent restoration has returned it to its early 19th-century appearance.

Decoration

Wyatville supplied draped curtains and reeded poles, and had his painter George Hutchinson gild the cornice and frieze. In 1963 the original wall panels of rose du Barry crimson silk damask were replaced by a crimson and gold wallpaper, which faded rapidly. By 2004, the 1830s silk fabric survived on the sofa alone. It had been patched over the years and was in such a sad state that it was decided to redecorate and reupholster the room throughout, restoring the 1830s scheme. Richard Humphries rewove the silk for the wall panels, curtains and seat furniture. The tassels and tiebacks were recreated on the basis of surviving fragments, and the woodwork, furniture and curtain poles were repainted and, as necessary, regilded. The Aubusson carpet, c.1830, was laid in the 1830s.

Pictures

On the left-hand wall hang portraits of the *1st Earl Brownlow* (1779–1853), painted by Sir Martin Archer Shee in 1835 in his uniform as Lord-lieutenant of Lincolnshire; and of his first wife, *Sophia* (1787/8–1814), by William Owen, 1813. On the east (far) wall are the 1st Earl's mother, *Frances* (1756–1847), at the age of 90 with her grandson, Lord Alford; and the 1st Earl's third wife, *Emma Sophia* (1792–1872), in 1826.

Furniture

18th-century kingwood *bureau plat* in the style of Charles Cressent (1685–1758), stamped.

17th-century *coffer* of speckled lacquer with sharkskin and mother-of-pearl inlay and silver mounts on a stand of about 1730.

The Breakfast Room

This room was until recently used as a private dining room. In 1809–10 Wyatville drew up plans for a 'Great Library' (now the Hondecoeter Room) and 'Ante Library' (the Breakfast Room) for the 1st Earl Brownlow. Both rooms were fitted with bookcases now in the 3rd Earl's Library upstairs. The walls were finished with a gilt plaster cornice and fluted band around the ceiling. Double doors in the centre of the east wall connect this room with the Red Drawing Room. The Egyptian-style marble fireplace also dates from the Wyatville period.

Pictures

Lord and Lady Tyrconnel in the Park at Belton of 1724–6 is Philippe Mercier's masterpiece and the outstanding picture at Belton. From left to right are: Tyrconnel (wearing the red sash of the Order of the Bath); the artist; Tyrconnel's cousin, Mrs Dayrell, on the swing; the invalid Lady Tyrconnel, being pushed in a bath chair by a black page; Francis Dayrell, looking at his wife; Tyrconnel's cousin, Savile Cust, pulling the rope; and Tyrconnel's brother, William.

The two mid-18th-century *views of Belton* displayed here record the grounds shortly after they were laid out in grand formal style by Lord Tyrconnel (see p. 37).

This bird's-eye view shows the extensive formal garden in the late 1740s, when Lord Tyrconnel was building the Belmount Tower (on the horizon at the end of the avenue)

George Romney painted the *1st Lord Brownlow* (1744–1807) for 36 guineas in 1779, four years before returning to paint the double-portrait of his wife *Frances* (1756/7–1847) and their eldest son *John, later 1st Earl Brownlow* (1779–1853). *The 1st Earl* appears again as a young man with his brother *Henry Cust* (1780–1861) in the full-length double-portrait by Hoppner of 1795 over the fireplace.

The melancholy figure of the 1st Earl's grandson *John, 2nd Earl Brownlow* (1842–67) was painted by G.F. Watts about 1865, when it was already clear that he was dying from tuberculosis. His poet friend Gerald Massey described 'The fine pale face, pathetically sweet, So thin with suffering that it seemed all soul', which is well caught in this portrait. Watts also painted *the 3rd Earl* (1844–1921) by the door to the Staircase.

Portraits of 20th-century Brownlows hang on the east (near) wall, including the *7th Lord Brownlow* (b. 1936), who generously gave the house, part of the contents and the garden to the National Trust in 1983.

Furniture

Mahogany *breakfast table*, c.1820. Five mid-18th-century mahogany *dining-chairs*. Pair of Regency mahogany *serving-tables*, in the style of the cabinetmaker Thomas Hope.

Ceramics

In the display cabinet is a collection of *English porcelain* from the Chelsea and Derby factories, including dishes in the shape of cabbage-leaves and sunflowers, mid-18th-century.

Clock

Regency clock, by Vulliamy.

The Hondecoeter Room

The Hondecoeter Room may have formed the upper part of the original kitchen. In 1808 the Cambridge architect Charles Humfrey was called in to carry out preliminary structural work, and in the following year Wyatville installed the 1st Earl Brownlow's library here.

(Above) The Hondecoeter Room

In 1876 the bookcases were removed upstairs, and the 3rd Earl introduced neo-Caroline panelling with moulded garlands, perhaps by W.G. Rogers, creating a state dining room as a fitting setting for the vast canvases by Melchior d'Hondecoeter which give the room its name. The present decoration revives that of the early 20th century, which had been suggested by Sir Edwin Lutyens.

Fireplace

This was brought from Ashridge Park.

Pictures

The major surviving set of decorative paintings by Melchior d'Hondecoeter (1636–95), who specialised in depicting flocks of birds in court-yard settings. All three are signed. We do not know where in the Low Countries these scenes were originally painted – or even if *Open land-scape with Poultry and Water-Fowl* originally

belonged with the other two scenes. Even before coming to Belton in 1873, they had been cut and adapted to fit another house in England. A fourth canvas could not be fitted in and is now in the US. The paintings were restored in 1985–90 at the Hamilton Kerr Institute.

Furniture

Early 19th-century mahogany *dining-table* and a pair of late Georgian mahogany drop-leaf dining-tables. Pair of late 19th-century silver *lamp bases* inscribed with texts celebrating the silver wedding anniversary of the 3rd Earl and Countess Brownlow in 1893.

The New Plate Room

This room was formerly the Serving Room. Built by the 3rd Earl in 1876 to provide direct access from the new state dining room to the kitchens, it is now used to display some of the remarkable collection of family silver.

Silver

The silver at Belton embodies the personal and
official high points in the history of the Brownlow
and Cust families, and although reduced from its
former splendour, is astonishingly rich and varied;
it is strongest at three periods – the late 17th
century, the 1760s and the Regency.

According to the 1698 inventory taken after
his death, Young Sir John had a handsome and
valuable collection of plate. It was headed by
his gold cup and personal cutlery, a luxury
normally found only at royal and noble tables.
His set of gilt display plate for the sideboard is
now represented by the water-bottles (also known
as pilgrim bottles). A generous provision of tableware demonstrates that in his dining habits, as in
his surroundings generally, Sir John kept up with
current fashion. Most of the elements of the late
Stuart dinner service were present – knives and
forks, 'boxes' for pepper, mustard and sugar, a set
of eight wrought salt cellars and a dozen plates.
His dessert silver was gilded. To supplement the
table display, a set of dish–
rings of pewter was
stored in the pantry.
Although the chocolate
pot (stored in the Still
House) was of base
metal, there was a
silver teapot for his
wife Alice's use and
a pestle, mortar and
skillet for cooking.

*The two-handled silver gilt cup of c.1725 is engraved with
the coat of arms of Viscount Tyrconnel*

*This decorative
water bottle
dated 1690 was
probably bought
by Young Sir
John Brownlow*

For their personal comfort there was a chamber-
pot and bedpan, and two sets of 'Dressing plate'.

Viscount Tyrconnel spent heavily on silver
following his first marriage in 1712. The two-
handled gilt cup, made c.1725 and engraved with
his arms, is characteristic of his taste for the solid,
massive *Régence* style of the second generation of
Huguenot silversmiths such as Paul de Lamerie.
As well as tureens, sauce boats, casters and
condiment vases, bread baskets and dish covers, he
had 'a depond for salad … with sconces', which
was a multiple object, presumably an *epergne* (or
table-centre) with interchangeable dishes and
candlebranches. For drinking he owned six
'solatares' (or wine coasters) as well as silver
labels for his wine bottles.

The silver collection was transformed
when Brownlow Cust became Speaker in
1761. The traditional issue of plate to the
Speaker consisted of 4,000 ounces of tableware
engraved with the royal arms and intended for
his official use. All the pieces are in a restrained late
rococo style, and their forms are characteristic of
contemporary Parisian silver. The most
spectacular item, the cistern with the royal arms
and supporters, was ordered in 1769, but not

delivered by Thomas Heming, the silversmith responsible for handling royal orders, until some months after the Speaker's death. The last of the traditional late Baroque cisterns to be made in England, it is unusual in not featuring the supporters of the owner. The service also included fish trowels, bottle stands and 'Urns for Sugar, Pepper and Mustard wth Ladles', as well as plates, dishes and covers, fish strainers and tureens.

The huge wine-cooler was made by the royal goldsmith Thomas Heming in 1770 for Speaker Cust

The impact of contemporary taste on the Belton plate can be seen vividly in the first two decades of the 19th century. From 1802 at least, the 1st Baron Brownlow was placing large orders with several goldsmiths, particularly the two leading retailers, Robert Garrard and Rundell, Bridge & Rundell. (The pieces by Paul Storr were ordered through the latter.) More significant for Belton was the opportunity Rundells and Garrards offered their clients to buy old silver. The Regency coincided with a marked revival of interest in an eclectic range of 'Old English' styles and in all forms of elaborate ornament, in reaction against the predominant Neo-classicism. Several of the Prince Regent's circle employed James Wyatt and his family, as at Belton, to reinterpret these styles, and silver was essential to dress such interiors. In 1808 the royal goldsmiths Rundell, Bridge & Rundell acquired from the King at their melt or bullion value many handsome pieces of the late Stuart furnishing silver that still remained in the royal palaces, such as chandeliers, sconces and firedogs. They astutely then sold them on for their full market value to a few special clients, such as William Beckford, the Duke of Buccleuch and Lord Brownlow.

An inventory taken in 1810 shows that there were by then eighteen sconces designated for the Chapel as well as seven for the Saloon, including the late Stuart ones from the royal collection. In 1819 Garrards purchased at Christie's six 'silver Girandoles' and overhauled sixteen second-hand sconces at a total cost of £111, adding 'Chasd Coronets' to four in acknowledgement of the recent elevation of Lord Brownlow to the earldom. Sconces were, of course, no novelty at Belton; there had been some in the 1690s, but the royal ones bought in the early 19th century are exceptionally rich in chased and cast ornament.

A sconce (wall-light) made for William and Mary and bearing their royal monogram on the back-plate. It was sold for scrap from the royal collection in 1808

The Old Kitchen

The Old Kitchen

Kitchens were created in this high chamber in 1808–10 to replace those in the north wing of the house, which were destroyed when Wyatville's Library and Ante-Library were built for the 1st Earl Brownlow. During the 20th century the kitchen returned to the basement of the house, and this room was abandoned.

The room today is a compilation of what remains of the early 19th-century kitchen (the table, cupboards, hatch and some of the utensils), and recently constructed evocations of what may have existed (the range and decoration). Look out for the set of fine monogrammed brass weights in their fitted box.

You leave the house to enter the West Court.

(Right) The gate screen

The Gate Screen

The magnificent Baroque gate screen opposite is one of three early 18th-century wrought-iron screens at Belton. It is attributed to John Warren, who provided a similar screen for Denham Place in Buckinghamshire (designed by William Stanton, who supervised the construction of Belton) in 1692.

The Stables (tea-room)

Although contemporary with the house, the stable block is noticeably less sophisticated. It is almost certainly the work of William Stanton.

The north end of the Stables contained twelve stalls on the east side, presumably for carriage horses; another six of a more rustic nature on the west side, which were possibly used for heavy horses; and eight loose boxes for riding horses. A large staff of grooms and coach-men lived above the stables, and straw, hay and other feed were also stored there. The hoist used for lifting them is still in the roof.

The Brewhouse

Across the entrance to the yard is the Brewhouse – designed by Jeffry Wyatville in the early 19th century, but substantially altered since his time – and a further three-bay coach-house. It now contains the shop and a display of carriages.

The little closed *invalid carriage* was built early in the 20th century for the 3rd Earl's wife, Lady Adelaide, who died in 1917. It was used to take the old lady for a sedate drive in the park, pulled by a pony and led by a groom.

The *wooden sleigh* is reputed to have been presented to the Brownlows by a Tsar of Russia in the 19th century. The present Lord Brownlow's sister, the Hon. Mrs Partridge, is an enthusiastic horsewoman, who had the invalid carriage restored and the sleigh painted in the 1960s, when the other two carriages were also acquired.

The late 19th-century *spider phaeton* was built by one of the finest London coach builders, Barker & Co. of Chandos Street. Phaetons were designed to be driven by the owner, and so the principal comfortable seat is at the front.

The canoe-bodied or Sefton *landau* was driven by a coachman. The easily raised and lowered hoods made it a versatile vehicle, suitable for all weathers.

Next to the Brewhouse is the former indoor riding school, used by the family for schooling horses. Its present roof was added during the Second World War.

(Right) The stables

The garden

Young Sir John's garden

The plan engraved by Hendrik Hulsbergh for Colen Campbell's *Vitruvius Britannicus* (1717) shows a highly developed scheme of formal parterres and walks to the north, south and east of the house. The main entrance to the south was approached through two courts: the first (F on Campbell's plan) had a circular drive that led into the second (G), a grid of paved walks crossing lawns ornamented with statues. To the south-east of this was a bowling green (E), while the north front looked out on to two elaborate parterres (B) bisected by a walk centred on an obelisk or fountain, and aligned with the main axis. Its boundary was marked then, as now, by the edge of the churchyard. To the west lay the kitchen garden (S) and orchards (V).

But the most dramatic scheme of all lay to the east. On the long axis of the house was the Great Pond (C), a canal constructed by John Holderness in 1685. This was flanked by close plantations shot through with symmetrical patterns of walks centred on *rond-points* in the style of the French garden designer André Le Nôtre (1613–1700), whose formalised arrangements of trees, water and planting had recently become highly fashionable in England. At the western end a small raised flower garden (D) gave access to the Chapel Drawing Room on the first floor of the house. Hulsbergh's engraving shows this surrounded by topiary trees, which also edged the *parterres de broderie* on the north side of the house. The garden and the park beyond were all enclosed by a five-mile wall in 1690.

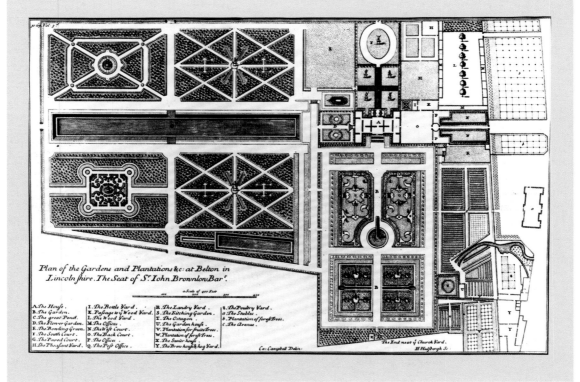

Plan of the Gardens and Plantations &c: at Belton in Lincolnshire. The Seat of Sʳ. Iohn Brownlow Barᵗ.

a Scale of 400 Feet

A. The House.
B. The Garden.
C. The great Pond.
D. The Flower garden.
E. The Bowling Green.
F. The South Court.
G. The Paved Court.
H. The Pheasant Yard.

I. The Bottle Yard.
K. Passage to ye Wood Yard.
L. The Wood Yard.
M. The Offices.
N. The West Court.
O. The Back Court.
P. The Offices.
Q. The Post Office.

R. The Landry Yard.
S. The Kitching Garden.
T. The Octagon.
U. The Garden house.
V. Plantation for fruite Trees.
W. Plantation of forest Trees.
X. The Senior house.
Y. The Brew house & hog Yard.

z. The Poultry Yard.
a. The Stables.
b. Plantation of forest Trees.
c. The Avenue.

The End next of Church Yard.

Ca: Campbell Delin.

H Hulsbergh Sc.

The development of the garden

As with any major Caroline country house, Belton required an appropriately elaborate setting, and Young Sir John Brownlow was already embarking on a dramatic transformation of the surrounding landscape as the first stone was being laid. In 1685 he planted no fewer than 21,400 ash trees and 9,500 oaks, along with 614 fruit trees, 260 limes, 2,000 roses and 100 gooseberry bushes. These new grounds may well have been laid out with advice from William Winde, who could also turn his hand to landscape design.

Young Sir John's nephew, Viscount Tyrconnel, made a number of innovations, building a heated greenhouse – where melons were cultivated and experiments conducted to see if pineapples could be grown – and creating the Wilderness to the west of the house with its cascade and picturesque ruins, which still survive (see below). The appearance of the garden in Tyrconnel's time can be seen in two paintings, which hang in the Breakfast Room, and in a bird's-eye view by Thomas Badeslade, made in the early 1750s. Badeslade's engraving also shows what was the most significant departure from the 17th-century layout, the replacing of the Great Pond by a long walk. This came about by accident rather than design. In May 1751 a sluice which drained the Great Pond was inadvertently closed, causing a disastrous flood. As a result, the pond was filled in.

In 1778 the 1st Lord Brownlow engaged the landscape gardener William Emes (1730–1803) to draw up a 'Plan of the park and of the Demesne lands at Belton … with some Alterations'. In the event, Emes's plans seem to have gone largely unexecuted, although his idea of a pleasure ground to the north of the house was approved, and the last of the parterres was removed to make way for it. In the east the formal 17th-century planting was thinned out, making the woods more naturalistic.

Lord Brownlow's son, the 1st Earl, made further changes, creating what is now known as the Italian Garden, with encouragement from his father-in-law Sir Abraham Hume.

The 3rd Earl Brownlow laid out the Dutch Garden and added box-edged parterres to the Italian Garden. The garden was edged with flowering shrubs, cherry, laburnum, may, viburnum, flowering currant, apple and pear. On either side of the Orangery were two parterres, one laid out as the Prince of Wales's feathers, and the other, to the west, as a series of small beds branching from a central vein. These were edged with box and planted with violas.

During the First World War many of the Belton flower-beds were turned over to the cultivation of fruit and vegetables, an enterprise which proved so successful that the 6th Lord Brownlow was able to say that 'the turnover of about £80 per month … is a model for an estate, although we only have four men'. The war effort also took the pergola from the fountain in the Italian Garden, as well as a box-and-yew maze which stood in the pleasure garden.

In recent times the 6th Lord Brownlow's second wife, Dorothy, planted the borders of the Dutch Garden with scarlet roses, while his third wife, Leila, preferred pink and white tea roses. The present Lady Brownlow replaced them with yellow and white roses and borders of lavender.

Since 1984 the National Trust has striven to maintain the traditionally high standard of gardening at Belton with a limited staff. It has also devoted time and money to restoring many of the key features of the garden, including the Orangery and the Exedra maze.

Peregrine Cust describes the great flood of 1751

'The side of the great pond broke & in less than an hour the water run out intirely it broke down the Garden wall near the Statue of Cain & Abell, travers'd the Garden, broke down the wall that parts that & the Kitchen Garden went thro the latter, broke down the wall facing the Water just below Manton's Mill & there emptied itself; it ran with prodigious force & velocity & has done great mischief having destroyed the produce of the Kitchen garden such as Melons Pease &c & filled the whole space it ran over with sand.'

The Italian Garden

In 1810 the 1st Earl commissioned Jeffry Wyatville to redesign the area to the north-east of the house, which had until then been occupied by the kitchen garden. Wyatville's plans show an elegant classical landscape, with a large south-facing conservatory (completed c.1820 and now known as the Orangery) next to the church, a circular 'bason' with a fountain (built in 1816), and a dairy in the form of a small temple. The dairy was never built, and its place was taken by Wyatville's Lion Exedra (or semi-circular screen), which was moved here in 1921.

The Dutch Garden

The Dutch Garden is approached either from the north terrace, or via the garden door which opened from the wing built in 1877 to connect the north-west corner of the house to the existing office block. Created in 1879, its layout was based on Hulsbergh's *Vitruvius Britannicus* engraving, and formed part of the 3rd Earl's neo-Caroline 'restoration' of Belton; it takes its name from the style of garden introduced to England from Holland in the late 17th century. Parterres lined the walk along the terrace, at either end of which were clipped box hedges and slatted wooden seats. There were originally 40 beds to each side of the central pathway, planted with aubrietia, arabis, grape hyacinth, phlox, primrose and auricula, while the stone cisterns were filled with tulips, violas and wallflowers. (The emphasis on spring blooms was due to the fact that the 3rd Earl and his wife rarely stayed at Belton during the summer months.) The golden and Irish yews were planted when the garden was laid out, as were the clipped yew hedges which neatly edge it.

Garden sculpture and ornaments

The central walk through the Dutch Garden leads to a limestone sundial in the form of Time with an attendant cherub. This was brought into the garden by Viscount Tyrconnel and is by the Danish carver Caius Gabriel Cibber (1630–1700), 'sculptor in ordinary unto His Majesty' William III. The bronze dial itself is modern.

Beyond the sundial, closing the axis of the mirror pond, is a figure of Ceres, dated 1850

The Italian Garden with the Orangery and church

(Above) The Dutch Garden

and the work of the Italian sculptor F. Franchi. A small Palladian summer-house, reputed to have been brought by the 1st Earl Brownlow from nearby Culverthorpe Hall, stands at the other end of the piece of water. Four 18th-century life-size Italian marble figures, including Neptune, Flora and Venus, adorn the Statue Walk, extending from the north terrace in front of the house, which may be those listed in the 1754 inventory as having stood on the turf on the south front of the house. Some of the bewildering array of ornamental urns and vases must date from the Wyatville era, but others, including the massive rectangular cisterns in the middle of the Dutch Garden, were introduced by the 3rd Earl in the late 19th century.

The church of SS Peter and Paul (*not National Trust*)

Evidence of the original Norman building still survives in the north arcade and the lower part of the west tower. The Perpendicular windows and the ceilings at the western end of the aisle are late medieval, while the upper tower bears the date 1638, the year in which it was rebuilt by Richard Brownlow. Virtually all of the rest of the church belongs to the 19th century. In 1816 the 1st Earl commissioned Jeffry Wyatville to design the chapel on the north side as a memorial to his first wife, Sophia Hume, who had died two years earlier.

The church has always been closely associated with the owners of Belton, and still contains a remarkable group of Brownlow and Cust monuments.

The park

In November 1690 William III's Secretary of State, the 2nd Earl of Nottingham, ordered the Solicitor General to prepare a Bill granting Young Sir John Brownlow the right to 'enclose and Impark such of his Lands in Belton Manthorpe and Londonthorpe … as he shall think fitt & Convenient for ye propertie not exceeding one Thousand Acers'. At the same time Young Sir John was also given the right to keep deer – something which he had apparently already been doing since at least 1686.

The earliest surviving map of the Belton estates dates from the time of this imparkment. It shows an area stretching from Peascliffe in the west to Ermine Street in the east. The great Eastern Avenue, which ran from the house along the same east–west axis as Young Sir John's Great Pond, is clearly visible, and may well date from before Richard Brownlow's purchase of Belton in the early 17th century – there is evidence to suggest that the oldest trees were planted about 1580.

The most dramatic architectural features of the park owed their origins to Viscount Tyrconnel, who between 1742 and 1751 introduced a picturesque Wilderness, a Gothick ruin and Cascade, and a prospect tower from which to enjoy his improvements to the landscape of Belton.

The resulting picturesque landscape – shown in a 1749 engraving by Francis Vivares – was described by Tyrconnel in a letter to his nephew and heir John Cust in April 1745: 'a grand Rustick arch finished with vast Rough Stones over ye Cascade of ye River, and two Huge Artificial Rocks on each side, Design'd and executed, as I think, in a taste superior to anything that I have see'.

In the course of the 19th century a small rustic summer-house (with a floor made from the knuckle-bones of deer) was built on the banks of the river, with a suitably rustic bridge leading to it, but both have since disappeared. During the Second World War the Wilderness was opened to the public, and in 1976 an adventure playground was built, with a miniature railway.

The Belmount Tower

The Belmount Tower was built between 1749 and 1751 by the master mason William Grey and the master builder and joiner Samuel Smith. It consisted of a tall arch flanked by two lower arches, supporting a single room reached by a spiral staircase, with a painted iron cupola topped by a gilded star and a wooden balustrade on a hipped roof.

The Cascade in the Wilderness

About 1742 Tyrconnel decided to exploit the potential of the River Witham to the west of the house, planting its valley with trees and shrubs, and draining the stream to create a waterfall, which was embellished with a Gothick ruin.

The picturesque cascade was created by Lord Tyrconnel in the Wilderness about 1742. He was so proud of the result that he sent copies of this engraving to his relations

The Belmount Tower

The Tower had a dual function. It terminated the Eastern Avenue, providing a focus to the vista from the house; and it served as a prospect tower from which Viscount Tyrconnel could enjoy views over his park. As such it became quite famous: after a visit to Belton in 1757, Mrs Philip Lybbe Powis recorded that 'from a temple in the garden called Belle Mount you may see seven counties at once, a thing from one spot thought very remarkable'. Near the Tower, on the south side of the avenue, there was a small plantation, Eleanor's Bower, named after Tyrconnel's first wife and created some time before the death in 1721 of her mother, Dame Alice Brownlow.

In the later 18th century, the 1st Lord Brownlow's brother-in-law, Philip Yorke, advised that 'Belmount … may be well clipped its two wings; they are the most offending members, and I think sh'd be cut off'. Brownlow apparently took Yorke's advice, since the arches have vanished, and today the Tower is supported by rather ugly buttresses. He also set about establishing plantations on the south side of the park, and by 1784 he had moved the main approach to Belton from the South Avenue to a new public road to the east, connecting with the village thoroughfare to the north of the house.

By the time of the 1st Lord Brownlow's death in 1807, the park had almost acquired the form that it retains today. The Grantham–Lincoln road which now forms its western boundary was built in 1804, and the Five Gates Road from Barkston Heath to Londonthorpe was completed, giving access between Belton and Londonthorpe.

The 1st Earl rebuilt the Keeper's Lodge on the north side of the Old Wood (a large plantation in the centre of the park), renovated the Gothick ruins over the Cascade, and called in the architect Anthony Salvin to design several summer-houses and a Tudoresque boathouse.

The 3rd Earl, who succeeded in 1867, planted specimen conifers in the Wilderness and Boathouse Plantation, and rhododendrons and yew walks in the latter. He also laid out the south side of the park as a golf course; this was seriously damaged during the First World War, when an army camp, served by a railway from Peascliffe to Belmount, was erected in the park.

Perhaps the most significant change to the park landscape since the 3rd Earl's death in 1921 was the felling of the South Avenue, which succumbed to Dutch Elm disease in the 1970s. The National Trust, assisted by the Kensington and Chelsea Association of Trust members, has replanted the whole avenue with Turkey oaks.

A father's farewell

Soon after the death in 1851 of the 1st Earl's son and heir, Viscount Alford, Richard Westmacott was commissioned to design a monumental pillar to be erected south of the grove of trees half-way between Towthorpe and the Old Wood (now in the golf course). The eight-foot high column, placed on a pedestal and surmounted by a vase garlanded with flowers, was completed in 1852. Its touching Latin inscription reads: 'Farewell my dearest son. Among these trees, once fortunate in aspect, offered in your name against a prayer, I, your unfortunate father, weeping, place this here.'

The first Brownlows at Belton

From the law to the land

Like the Hobarts of Blickling, the Harpurs of Calke and the Phelipses of Montacute, the first Brownlows of Belton owed their fortune to the rapid expansion of the legal profession during the later 16th century – and, like those families, they were quick to acquire a country estate with the proceeds of their law work and to establish themselves as landed gentry.

Richard Brownlow

Richard Brownlow (1553–1638), who laid the foundations of the family's wealth, was the son of a successful London lawyer with a substantial house in High Holborn, near the present Brownlow Street. After entering Clement's Inn, Richard was admitted to the Middle Temple in 1583; and just seven years later he was appointed to the important and lucrative office of Chief Prothonotary of the Common Pleas, with a spectacular annual salary of £6,000.

Brownlow made good use of his wealth, setting up his family at a country house in Enfield, and putting a high proportion of his income into land, much of it in Lincolnshire. Perhaps attracted by the presence of relations in the Isle of Axholme, in about 1598 he bought Ringston Hall at Rippingale and lands at Kirkby Underwood, to the south-east of Grantham, from Sir Thomas Coney. Brownlow also paid high prices for other estates in Lincolnshire: in December 1600 Henry Pakenham sold him a considerable estate at Gosberton and Surfleet, just north of Spalding, for £2,120. And in 1603 Brownlow began to negotiate the purchase of another of Pakenham's holdings – the manor of Belton, two miles to the north of Grantham.

Details of Belton's earlier history are rather sparse. There may well have been a manor house here prior to the 16th century, although according to tradition, a subsequent owner built a new one on or near the site of the present

Orangery, close by the church of SS Peter and Paul; only the gate-piers in the north wall by the Orangery survive.

In 1609 Pakenham agreed that Belton should revert to Richard Brownlow for £4,100, after his own and his wife's death. Eight years later, the Pakenhams entertained James I here during the King's progress from Burley-on-the-Hill to Lincoln. This honour so impoverished them that they resigned their life interest in Belton in 1619, Richard agreeing to pay them an annuity of £560 during both their lives.

During the 1620s and '30s Richard and Katherine Brownlow rarely visited Belton, preferring to live at Enfield. The only architectural contribution which Richard made to the property – or at least, the only contribution to survive – was the rebuilding of the church tower in 1638, the year of his death. Of the couple's six children, their eldest son, John, born in 1588, died young. Their second, born in 1594, was christened Anthony, but renamed John after his brother's death. A third son, William, was born in 1595. There were also three daughters, Elizabeth, Mary and Audrey.

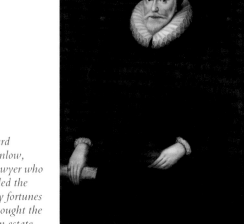

Richard Brownlow, the lawyer who founded the family fortunes and bought the Belton estate

'Old Sir John' Brownlow

Richard Brownlow's two surviving sons were both married in 1621, John to Alice, daughter of Sir John Pulteney, and William to Elizabeth, daughter and co-heiress of William Duncombe. At the same time their father settled on his eldest son the bulk of the family estates, including Belton, Ringston, Kirkby Underwood and Rippingale, while William was given property in London and Leicestershire. Both boys followed their father into the law, via Oxford and the Inner Temple, and both were made baronets by Charles I in 1641.

Sir John (1594–1679) – always known in the family as 'Old Sir John', to distinguish him from the builder of Belton House, 'Young Sir John' – seems to have led a quiet and leisurely existence, dividing his time between Belton, Lennox House in Drury Lane, and a house which he bought by the Thames at Isleworth. He carried on his father's policy of investing heavily in land, becoming a substantial sheep farmer at a time when enclosure made this a highly profitable business. Through shrewd planning and careful management he was able to more than double his inheritance, which even at the outset provided him with a healthy £4,000 a year.

But Old Sir John and his wife had no children of their own, and their nephews – his brother's sons, Richard, William, John and Benjamin, and his sister Elizabeth's son, Richard Sherard – became the focus of their attention. In 1647 Old Sir John went to great lengths to reach a settlement dividing his property among them, and after Richard Sherard's death in 1668 the couple adopted his eldest daughter Alice, bringing her to live with them at Belton and giving her a good education. Throughout their lives Sir John's nephews and nieces and their families received presents of money from a large stock hidden away in sacks in each of his three houses.

A marriage is arranged

Like his father before him, Old Sir John was a long liver, and one by one his nephews, of whom he had such high hopes, died. By November 1675 he was lamenting that he had

'Old Sir John' and Alice, Lady Brownlow. They had no children, and so passed the estate to their grand-nephew, 'Young Sir John'

'only two kinsmen left of my name and blood' – his two great-nephews Young Sir John (1659–97) and William (1665–1702), grandsons of his brother Sir William. Worried that the Brownlow family might soon die out altogether, the old man took charge of his eldest great-nephew, John, whose father had died in 1668, sending him to Westminster School and bringing him to live at Isleworth and the Drury Lane house. Both there and at Belton Young Sir John must often have found himself in the company of his cousin Alice Sherard; and at the end of 1675 Old Sir John added a codicil to his will expressing his earnest desire that a marriage should be effected 'between my kinsman Sir John Brownlow, Bt, and my kinswoman Alice Sherard in case they shall affect one another'.

The young people were evidently favourites with their great-uncle, and the idea of a marriage to unite the two branches of the family must have been conceived fairly early on. Luckily, they did 'affect one another' – Alice was certainly a very willing partner, according to a little notebook kept by her. On 27 March 1676 the couple, both scarcely sixteen years old, were married in Henry VII's Chapel at Westminster Abbey, and to mark the event Old Sir John gave his great-nephew a gold watch and chain which had cost him £17, and complementary wedding rings worth £25. Lady Brownlow also spent £6 having a portrait painted of Young Sir John, probably as a present to Alice, her goddaughter. Three years later Old Sir John was dead, and the young couple inherited the bulk of his considerable fortune.

Building the house

'Young Sir John' and Dame Alice Brownlow

Equipped with their great-uncle's considerable fortune – £20,000 in ready money and an income of around £9,000 a year – Young Sir John and Dame Alice Brownlow soon set aside the tradition of thrift and simple living which had underpinned and nurtured the family's rising fortunes for nearly a century. They launched into London society, spending £5,000

'Young Sir John' Brownlow, the builder of the house

on a new house in Southampton (now Bloomsbury) Square, laid out in the 1660s by the 4th Earl of Southampton, and one of the most fashionable areas of the capital. And, inevitably, they turned their thoughts to the creation of a new country house which would be an appropriate setting for their rank and wealth. To design it, Sir John seems to have turned to the soldier-architect William Winde.

William Winde

Winde (d. 1722) was the son of a royalist who had fled to the Low Countries after the Civil War, dying a lieutenant-colonel in the service of the States of Holland in 1658. He followed in his father's footsteps, becoming an ensign in command of English troops at Bergen-op-Zoom and, on his return to England in 1660, buying a commission in the King's Troop of the Royal Regiment of Horse.

Winde seems from quite early on to have taken an active interest in military engineering. When the Dutch fleet lay in the Thames in June 1667, he assisted in the fortification of Gravesend Reach. He had for some years been pursuing a parallel career as a country house architect, largely as the result of the patronage and encouragement of his godfather, William, 1st Earl of Craven. The Earl commissioned Winde to take on the design of his house at Hampstead Marshall in Berkshire, and perhaps also that of Ashdown, a hunting lodge on the downs twelve miles away and now the property of the National Trust. In 1682–5 Winde also remodelled another of Craven's country houses, Combe Abbey in Warwickshire.

There are several reasons for attributing the design of Young Sir John Brownlow's new house at Belton to Winde. The most telling is the stylistic parallel between Belton and the west front of Combe Abbey. There is also a letter written in February 1690, soon after Belton was completed, in which Winde recommended Edward Goudge to his patron and kinswoman

Lady Bridgeman, saying that the plasterer 'is now looked on as ye beste master in Ingland in his profession, as his worke att Coombe, Hampsted, & Sr. John Brownloe's will evidence'. Goudge also worked with Winde on the alterations to Craven's Drury House, and it is tempting to speculate that the architect may have been brought to Brownlow's attention by Craven himself, since the Earl was a neighbour of Old Sir John in Drury Lane. But if Winde was the architect of Belton House, his involvement probably went no further than providing 'a design of it in paper, though but roughly drawn', in the words of the influential architect Roger Pratt.

William Stanton

The execution and general supervision of the project were left to the mason-contractor William Stanton (1639–1705). A member of a family of masons and sculptors with a yard near St Andrew's church, Holborn, in London (which in 1684 he contracted to rebuild with the decorative carver Edward Pierce – another of Winde's collaborators), Stanton was primarily a monumental sculptor. He probably came to Brownlow's notice in 1681, when he was paid £100 to set up a monument in Belton parish church to Old Sir John and his wife Alice. But in common with many 17th-century mason-sculptors, he not only undertook building work, but was also prepared to act as clerk of works and general site supervisor when the occasion arose. Stanton is also thought to have designed several country houses on his own account – one of which, Denham Place in Buckinghamshire (1701), closely resembles Belton. The large sum of money which he received at Belton – some £5,000 at intervals over a three-year period between March 1685 and May 1688 – indicates that he and his assistant John Thompson (who went on in the latter year to work as contractor for Wren on St Paul's) played a central role in both the organisation of the scheme and the construction of the house.

How much Belton owes to Winde, and how much to Stanton, is impossible to say. No doubt the original drawings were revised and modified both by Stanton himself and by the various craftsmen responsible for the detailed work.

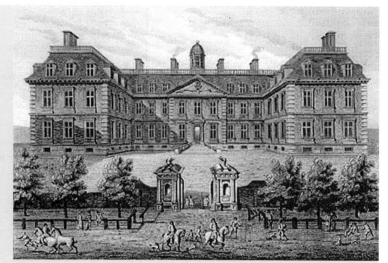

The inspiration: Clarendon House

The design of Brownlow's new house is ultimately based on the spectacular palace at the top of St James's Street, Piccadilly, which Roger Pratt designed in 1664–7 for the Lord Chancellor, Edward Hyde, 1st Earl of Clarendon. In 1683, after Hyde's death, it was sold to 'certaine rich bankers and mechanics', who demolished it and redeveloped the site, but during its short life Clarendon House's elegant symmetry and confident and commonsensical design made it one of the most admired buildings in England. And it is at Belton that the Clarendon type achieves its purest and arguably its greatest incarnation.

(Above) The south front, painted about 1720 (West Stairs)

Building Belton

Preparations for the new house began in
February 1684, when the steward's accounts
show the first of many payments to local
workers for gathering gorse and bracken, and
binding them in sheaves as fuel to fire the brick
clamps, or kilns, which were being set up on the
site. Temporary buildings were put up, and – in
a gesture which suggests that Young Sir John
had inherited at least some of the old Brownlow
thrift – the old manor house was carefully taken
down, and wood, stone, glass, lead and slates
were stored ready to be reused in the new
building. Reused Jacobean panelling and a door-
case in the attics bear witness to this frugality. At
the same time Sir John's workmen stripped and
dismantled Ringston Hall, also left to him by his

great-uncle, and 289 loads of stone, slate and
wood were carted the twelve miles north-west
to Belton at a cost of £189. On 13 May 1684
Brownlow's brickmaker, Samuel Truman, was
given a shilling 'to drinck at the bourning the
first Clamp'. However, within a few months
Truman was dead, and Robert Broughton
and William Plumridge had replaced him –
probably, like him, itinerant brickmakers who
moved on to nearby Belton Heath and set up
their own clamps and diggings for the duration
of the works. Between April 1685 and July 1686
the two men, together with several other less
important contractors, supplied just over
1,750,000 bricks, for walling, outbuildings and
the carcase of the house itself.

As that carcase took shape, the site must
have been a hive of activity. Wagonload after
wagonload of the golden Ancaster stone which
was used to face the house was brought over

from the nearby Heydour quarries of Samuel Marsh. Stone for the quoins and keystones came from Ketton, outside Stamford.

On 23 March 1685, the steward recorded that he 'Gave the mason to drinck att laying the first Ston on the new house, 5s'. Once begun, construction work progressed quite quickly, although apparently not quickly enough for Brownlow, since two months later his steward 'Gave the Rasers of Ston to drinck to make hast 1s 6d'. This seems to have done the trick. Stanton had the shell erected and probably roofed by the autumn of 1686, when slate, wainscot and floorboards were being brought in, and decoration and finishing were well in hand by the following year. A receipt in the family archives, undated, but probably from 1687 or 1688, shows that the carpenter Edward Willcox received £90 'for making ye Lanthorne and rails and Ballisters on ye plattforme', and a further twelve guineas for 'boarding on ye platforme balustrade and cupola'. In November 1688 Sir John and Lady Brownlow moved in.

Planning

As at Clarendon House, the main storey of Belton is set above a half-basement, echoing Pratt's advice that 'an ascent is most graceful with such a basement for it looks like a thing complete in itself, and this adds to the height and majesty of a building; and a prospect is more pleasant to a house than where none, as must necessarily fall out where we cannot see over the top of our out-walls'. By siting the kitchen, buttery, larder, servants' hall and other domestic offices in this basement, Winde

and Stanton left the two main floors free to be devoted to family lodgings and state apartments, with the servants' lodgings placed up in the attic storey and reached via sets of back stairs at either end of the house – a comparatively recent innovation which had been pioneered by Pratt at Coleshill in Berkshire.

The visual and ceremonial focus of the house was the group of four chambers at its centre, emphasised on both of the main façades by three-bay pedimented projections. On the ground floor of the south front, the Marble Hall led into a great parlour to the north (now the Saloon). Above the Marble Hall a great chamber (now the Library, but called the 'great dining room' in an inventory drawn up when the Brownlows moved in in 1688) stood back-to-back with the state bedchamber and its closet (now the Queen's Bedroom and Ante-Library). The other main rooms, including the Brownlows' own lodgings on the first floor and a series of reception rooms below, were symmetrically disposed to either side of this group, the only jarring note being the placing of the main staircase to the east of the single-storey hall.

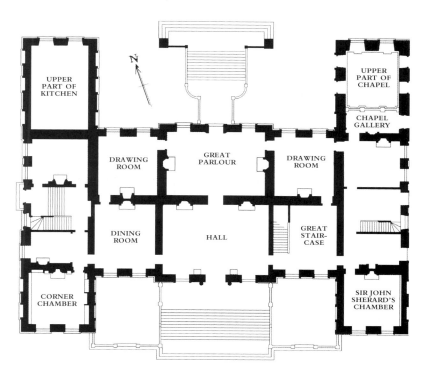

(Right) The ground floor with the room names in use in 1688

Plasterwork and wood carvings

But any qualms about the asymmetry of the Staircase Hall are more than assuaged by Edward Goudge's masterly ceiling, incorporating the Brownlow crest of a greyhound in the corner cartouches, bordered by scrolling sunflowers and with a garland of fruit and flowers. In Young Sir John's time, the Staircase Hall had a three-fold function, as the ceremonial route of ascent to the great dining room, a recreation area and a picture gallery: the 1688 inventory shows that it held a billiard table, 'Two Sticks wth balls & Jacks' and 'Three & fortie pictures all Gold Gilt frames some being large'.

The two wings contained lodgings for Dame Alice's relations, the Sherards, and nurseries for the Brownlows' daughters, to the south; and a kitchen and chapel to the north. This chapel, again with plasterwork by Goudge, is not only one of the least altered of the 17th-century interiors at Belton; it is also a *tour de force* of Caroline decoration, a secular masterpiece in

The Marble Hall carvings in the style of Grinling Gibbons

which spirituality gives way to the display of wealth. Lush circlets and scrolls of acanthus leaves, fruit and flowers, all swirl around putti who cavort with Baroque exuberance among foliage, grapes and flowers, while four trios of chubby – and somewhat surly – cherub heads sing out from high-relief panels. The scene is presided over by two further putti who perch precariously on top of a magnificent Corinthian reredos, probably the work of Stanton (who provided the marble pavement and altar steps) and the local carver Edmund Carpenter.

Carpenter, whose only documented work is at Belton, was responsible for much of the woodcarving in the house. His bill, dated 26 March 1688, specifically mentions three chimneypieces, including one 'in the greate Parlor with fruit and flowers', for which he was paid £18, and another costing £26 10s, a 'very rich Chimny peece in the wth drawing roome To the great Parlor don wth varieties of fish and sheals [shells] With birds foulige fruit & flowers'. Many of the Belton carvings have since been rearranged, and this last probably refers to

Edward Goudge's plasterwork ceiling in the Chapel

the right-hand overmantel now decorating the Marble Hall. Other carvings have traditionally been assigned to Grinling Gibbons. Carpenter's overmantels in the Saloon and the Marble Hall both have partners that are clearly not by his hand: these are much bolder and more finely executed, and certainly show close affinities with Gibbons's authenticated work.

Furnishings

The 1688 inventory shows that Belton was furnished in a fairly simple but modern manner. The parlour was furnished with 'two very large seeing glasses', 'three crimson sarcenet curtains fringed about', eighteen rush chairs and two japanned tables. The first-floor state bedchamber contained 'one fine bedstead with green damask curtains and valance … twelve green velvet armchairs … and three pieces of Moses tapestry hangings'.

By 1698, when a second inventory was taken, Young Sir John and Dame Alice had had time to install some more opulent and fashionable decoration. In August 1691, for example, Brownlow commissioned John Vanderbank, the Chief Arras Worker of the Great Wardrobe, to make a set of hangings for the drawing room adjoining the family gallery in the Chapel, which were 'to be of Indian figures according to ye pattern of the Queens wch are at Kensington and to be finished as well in every kind or else the said Sr John Brownlowe shall not bee obliged to have theme'. These hangings, which

are still in the Chapel Drawing Room, were modelled on Mogul miniatures which had recently been brought back from India.

The richer decorative scheme of which Vanderbank's tapestries formed a part was carried through into the rest of the house, if the newly named rooms listed in the 1698 inventory are anything to go by. Now there were a 'green damask drawing room', a 'white varnished drawing room' and a 'white gilt closet', a 'white and green painted chamber', a 'blue and white painted chamber' and a 'Scotch plaid room'.

A mysterious death

But by 1698 Sir John Brownlow was dead. The serious, rather smug young man, shown complete with double chin in John Riley's portrait of about 1685 in the Saloon, had done everything expected of a wealthy country gentleman. He had built himself an appropriately grand new house; he had served as High Sheriff of Lincolnshire and MP for Grantham. Everything seemed set for the young man's further advancement, perhaps even a peerage. But in July 1697, a contemporary reported that 'Sir John Brownlow member of Parliament for Grantham … last week shot himself at Mr Freakes [his uncle's house] in Dorsetshire, but the reason not known'. The reason is still not known.

Young Sir John's widow stayed on at Belton until her death in 1721, spending her time in arranging advantageous matches for their daughters. According to her monument by Christopher Horsnaile the elder in Belton church, 'she was chiefly employed in their education: three of them she disposed in marriage to three noble peers of the realm [Jane to the future 2nd Duke of Ancaster, Elizabeth to the 6th Earl of Exeter, and Alice to the future 2nd Baron Guilford] and the fourth [Eleanor] to the husband's nephew, out of respect to his memory'. And, the inscription might have added, out of respect for that nephew's inheritance. For on Young Sir John's death Belton passed to his brother William, whose eldest son, another John, was that nephew and succeeded four years later, in 1702.

The 18th century

Sir John Brownlow III, Viscount Tyrconnel
A man of 'nice taste'

Young Sir John Brownlow's nephew, Sir John Brownlow III (1690–1754), has come down to us as rather a pathetic figure. He was possessed of a driving political ambition, but few political skills, and had an inordinately high opinion of his own importance (an opinion which was not shared by his family, his colleagues or his peers). His pretensions and his failure to achieve high office have tended to obscure a more positive side to his character – what one contemporary described as 'his nice taste and his well chosen knowledge' of the arts. It was this nice taste and well-chosen knowledge which were his greatest legacy to Belton.

In 1713, the year after Lady Brownlow had successfully engineered his marriage to her youngest daughter Eleanor, Sir John entered Parliament in the Whig interest as MP for Grantham. In the following year he was elected member for Lincolnshire, a seat which he held until 1722, when he was again returned for Grantham; and in 1718 he was created Viscount Tyrconnel and Baron Charleville, as a reward for supporting the Government, probably through the patronage of John Aislabie, Chancellor of the Exchequer. As an Irish peer, he was still able to sit in the Commons, and he continued to represent Grantham until his retirement in 1741. But in spite of his lengthy political career he made little mark.

For the first few years of their married life Eleanor and John divided their time between their town house in Arlington Street, St James's, and Bruton in Somerset. Viscount Tyrconnel's own inheritance, which included the Bruton property, provided him with a reasonable income, while his wife brought with her around £1,200 a year and a fourth share in her father's unsettled estates. But Tyrconnel (or rather Sir John Brownlow, as he still was at that time) was a bad manager and proved unable to live within his means. To be fair, this was partly because he had inherited an encumbered estate from a father who had died intestate. But the couple's difficulties were exacerbated by his love of ostentatious display, which put a great deal of pressure on the family resources. In 1715 self-imposed economies obliged the family to shut up the Arlington Street house, and Eleanor retired to Bruton with a household of six servants and a dog called Brill. And then in 1721 Eleanor's mother, Alice, died, and under the terms of a settlement made by Old Sir John on

Viscount Tyrconnel proudly wears his robes as a knight of the Order of the Bath. He hoped for, but did not receive, an English peerage

Young Sir John's marriage 45 years earlier, Belton passed to them, becoming their main residence.

The Tyrconnels immediately began to consolidate their Lincolnshire estates, buying back some of the Brownlow property which had been bequeathed to Eleanor's sisters. Despite their efforts, the Belton estate remained a shadow of its former self: it gave the Tyrconnels an income of only £4,000, half of what Old Sir John Brownlow had received in the 17th century. However, the couple were far from poor, and Viscount Tyrconnel felt free to indulge his love of the arts. Inspired perhaps by the aesthete Frederick, Prince of Wales, with whom he was on friendly terms, he patronised the poet Alexander Pope, the sculptor Henry Cheere, and artists of the calibre of Thomas Smith of Derby, the court portrait-painter Charles Jervas, and Philippe Mercier, whose delightful conversation piece of the Tyrconnels relaxing in the grounds of Belton – one of the first pictures of its kind to be painted in England – now hangs in the Breakfast Room. Tyrconnel also began the collection of Old Masters which eventually found their way to Belton from his Arlington Street house and some of which can still be seen in the Blue Dressing Room.

Belton in Tyrconnel's time

Inventories – this time from 1737 and 1754 – and bills are again our major source of information about Belton's appearance during Viscount Tyrconnel's time.

The Saloon, then still known as the great parlour, remained one of the most important chambers in the house, and Tyrconnel lavished a good deal of money on its decoration and furnishing. In 1729 he paid 15 guineas to have the room gilded by Mark Antony Hauduroy, who had worked at Knole in Kent for the 1st Duke of Dorset in 1723–4. In 1737 the great parlour contained the six family portraits which hang there today: Tyrconnel's father and mother, and his uncle and aunt, Young Sir John and Dame Alice, all by Riley and Closterman; and two attributed to Henry Tilson of his cousins and sisters-in-law – Jane Brownlow,

who married the 2nd Duke of Ancaster, and Margaret, who died tragically on the eve of her wedding. The furniture included 'two large pier glasses with three brass sconces to each' and 'two marble tables'. These pier-glasses and their matching tables are among the most important pieces in the house today. Bought by Tyrconnel, and showing the Viscount's arms set in broken pediments, they may perhaps have been designed by William Kent.

Most notable among the furnishings of what is now the Red Drawing Room, immediately west of the Saloon, were 'two pieces of fine tapestry hangings with the Late Lord's Arms and the history of Diogenes and Plato'. These were part of a set of four tapestries illustrating scenes from the life of the philosopher Diogenes and were probably woven at Mortlake. The other two may perhaps have been kept at Tyrconnel's Arlington Street house, and the full set is now in the Tapestry Room at Belton.

As well as acquiring new hangings, paintings, books and other furnishings, the Tyrconnels changed the functions of several of the state rooms at Belton. Young Sir John Brownlow's state bedchamber over the great parlour (now the Queen's Bedroom) was turned into a picture gallery, while the room below it, the 'drawing room next to the greate Parlour' (now the Tyrconnel Room) was fitted out with a splendid bed of crimson damask, and filled with rich furniture, ornamental china figures and family portraits. In 1754 these items were valued at £250 5s, making it the most expensively furnished bedroom in the house.

In spite of his refined taste and his enthusiastic pursuit of learning, Viscount Tyrconnel seems to have inspired little in the way of admiration among his contemporaries. George II felt that he lacked wisdom and principle, calling him 'a puppy that never votes twice together on the same side'. The indefatigable letter-writer Mrs Delany, whom the Viscount wooed after Eleanor's death in 1730, felt that even though 'he had so vast a fortune, a title and was a good natured man … money without worth could not tempt her'. 'He had the character, very justly, of being silly', she said, 'and I would not tie myself to such a character for an empire.'

Anne Cust (in blue) with her children. In the centre in the embroidered waistcoat is her son John, to whom she passed Belton on inheriting it from her brother, Lord Tyrconnel; painted by Enoch Seeman (West Stairs)

The Custs

Finding an heir

Undaunted in his search for a new wife and a son to carry on the line – he and Eleanor had had no children – Tyrconnel soon found a less discerning object for his marital ambitions, in the person of Elizabeth Cartwright of Marnham. The couple were married in January 1732, although the match was resented by other members of the family, who were no doubt as keen to see Tyrconnel die childless as he was to father an heir. The cool reception was led by his surviving sister Anne, wife of Sir Richard Cust. Her husband, perhaps sharing Anne's disappointment, wrote to her in 1732 that her brother had sold himself to a devil. He and the new Lady Tyrconnel had just spent an evening together, 'with as much ease and pleasantry as could be expected from one that detested her'.

However, Elizabeth worked hard to appease her husband's family, and eventually won them over. In the event, the couple had no children of their own – a factor which may have played a part in softening the Custs' hearts. When Sir Richard died in 1734, leaving Anne to bring up their nine children, Tyrconnel and his wife, like the childless Old Sir John and Dame Alice Brownlow before them, focused their attention and ambitions on their nephews and nieces. The Cust family moved into a town house in nearby Grantham, where the Tyrconnels were constant visitors. Most of the Viscount's aspirations centred on his eldest nephew John (1718–70). In 1742 he found a bride for Sir John (as the latter became when he inherited his father's Pinchbeck baronetcy). She was a young heiress with £60,000, named Etheldred Payne, and in spite of some opposition from the Payne family, who thought that neither the Cust pedigree nor the Cust fortune was a match for theirs, the wedding took place in 1743.

Tyrconnel also used his influence to advance his nephew's political career. Having arranged his admission to the Middle Temple, where

Cust took chambers in 1739, he used his interest to ensure his nephew's election in 1743 as MP for Grantham, a seat which Cust held until his death, and did everything he could to promote his political career. That career proved to be considerably more distinguished than his uncle's: he was appointed Clerk of the Household to the Princess of Wales in 1751, and ten years later was elected Speaker of the Commons.

Tyrconnel never lived to see the full extent of his nephew's achievement, dying in 1754. To the end, his ambitions for Cust were tied up with his own desperate desire for the ultimate honour of a United Kingdom peerage, and he constantly pressed for the young man to raise the matter in the right quarters. But Cust seems to have been as shrewd and diplomatic in his private life as he was in politics, and humoured his uncle without ever doing a great deal to achieve the long-desired end. The Viscount led everyone to believe that he 'always despis'd Posthumous Pageantry', but, true to form, his funeral procession was a splendid affair, consisting of two armorial banner rolls, pairs of spurs and gauntlets, a standard and a helmet, shield and sword. Besides the family mourners, there were some 50 retainers.

Viscount Tyrconnel, like his father, died intestate. His sister Anne Cust succeeded to his estates and half of his possessions, and moved her family into Belton, making over the Grantham house to Sir John. However, he rarely used it, staying instead with his mother when he was not in London. In 1766, realising that he needed a country house appropriate to his dignity as Speaker of the House, she gave Belton to him – much to the chagrin of his brothers and sisters – and went back to Grantham.

Speaker Cust thought of retiring from his post to live the life of a country gentleman, but decided against it. He was re-elected in 1768 – the year in which the radical John Wilkes returned to England and entered Parliament for Middlesex, only to be expelled for accusing the government of instigating the massacre in St George's Fields in which the military had fired on a large crowd that had assembled to escort Wilkes to the House. Partly as a result of the controversies surrounding Wilkes, during the late 1760s Cust was called on to preside over what proved to be one of the stormiest periods in British parliamentary history. When he died in 1770, aged 51, his monument in Belton church attributed his death to the 'unusual fatigues of his office', brought about by 'the extraordinary increase of national business'.

(Right) Sir John Cust as Speaker of the House of Commons; by Sir Joshua Reynolds (Saloon)

Sir Brownlow Cust, 1st Lord Brownlow, who commissioned James Wyatt to modernise the house

Sir Brownlow Cust, 1st Baron Brownlow

Cust had little time to have any real impact on Belton. It was left to his son, Brownlow Cust (1744–1807), to make the first major architectural changes to the house since it had been built. Raised to the peerage in 1776 as Baron Brownlow as a reward for his father's distinguished political service, he was in a good position to do so. His first wife, Jocosa Drury, who died of 'putrid fever' in 1772 after two years of marriage, was worth £103,000. His second, Frances Bankes, the daughter of a wealthy London merchant, brought with her a further £100,000 when they married in 1775. The house

The north front after Wyatt had removed the rooftop balustrade and cupola

which Brownlow inherited must have seemed rather old-fashioned, in spite of his great-uncle's refurnishing and rearrangement of rooms. Brownlow quickly set about a programme of alterations and repairs.

James Wyatt transforms Belton

While all the repairs and redecoration work were being carried out, Brownlow was considering some more far-reaching changes to the structure of Belton. In March 1776, two months before his elevation to the peerage, he consulted a young man who was within a few years to become the most fashionable designer in the country, James Wyatt (1746–1813). Wyatt may well have been recommended by Philip Yorke of Erddig in Denbighshire, who was married to Brownlow's sister Elizabeth: the architect had been employed on some alterations to Erddig in 1773–4. The architect's astonishingly cavalier attitude towards his clients and his legendary lack of organisational skills had not yet tarnished his reputation, and Brownlow's choice and the timing of it suggests that he was eager to acquire the services of a distinguished architect who would transform Belton into an appropriate residence for a new peer.

As far as the exterior was concerned, that transformation involved the removal of those features which most obviously fixed the house as a creation of the late 17th century – the

balustrade on the roof and the cupola (which had in any case begun to leak). The roof was renewed in Westmorland slate; the alternating triangular and segmental pediments to the dormer windows were flattened, and the dormers themselves were reduced from eight to six on both fronts and given sash-windows; and the windows on the return walls of the south front were blocked and transformed into shallow niches. Wyatt also designed a new frontispiece for the main entrance door on the south front. The overall effect of Wyatt's changes to the exterior was to give Belton the appearance of a Caroline house which had been half-heartedly remodelled in a forlorn attempt to bring it into line with mid-Georgian taste – which was exactly what it was.

Internally, Wyatt's work was much less half-hearted, and as a result much more successful. The first of the four rooms which he redecorated was a first-floor bedchamber on the south front of the house (now the Boudoir). In 1776–7 this was converted into a dressing room for Lady Brownlow. It remains one of the few feminine rooms in what is otherwise a distinctly masculine house, and it is tempting to speculate that Lord Brownlow's second wife (they had been married for only a year) may well have had a say in its redecoration.

Next door to the Boudoir, Wyatt turned the old great dining chamber into an airy classical drawing room, giving it a shallow vaulted ceiling of enlarged coffer design, which survives. The process of raising the ceiling entailed cutting into two of the attic rooms, which were done away with, and diverting the old attic passage around it.

Wyatt remodelled two other rooms at Belton: the Yellow Bedroom, a first-floor bedchamber in the south-east wing; and the Blue Bedroom immediately below it, where today Wyatt's frieze and chimneypiece are overshadowed by the towering state bed, which was probably installed later.

Lord Brownlow's modernisation of Belton continued until the end of the century. Throughout the late 1770s and '80s John Langwith was employed, not only in implementing some of Wyatt's alterations, but also on

Wyatt's Neo-classical ceiling in the Boudoir

a host of other jobs, from hanging new sashes and putting up pictures to laying new floors and 'oltering a Bell in drawing room & Caseing ye Wier to Bells in Passage'.

At the same time, Brownlow was installing stoves and a water closet in the house, buying new furniture and adding to the already distinguished collection of paintings. He commissioned portraits of both his wives, from Benjamin West and Catherine Read, and acquired through his marriage to Frances Bankes an important group of pictures, mainly by artists of the Northern Schools. Like his relative Philip Yorke of Erddig, in the early 1770s he patronised the popular cabinetmaker Thackwaite ('Chair Work & Upholstery Work in General, at Reasonable Rates'), as well as purchasing over a thousand pounds worth of furniture from the Prussian ambassador Count Maltzan in 1771. By the time of Brownlow's death in 1807, Belton had been well and truly dragged into the 19th century, its surviving Caroline decoration somewhat at odds with the elegance and convenience of its Georgian interiors. But there were more changes to come.

The 19th century

John, 1st Earl Brownlow
Autocrat and aesthete

The new owner of Belton was the 1st Lord Brownlow's eldest son John (1779–1853), who in 1815 was created Earl Brownlow and Viscount Alford. As with so many of his class who reached manhood in the years following the French Revolution, the memory of rebellion abroad and the prospect of insurrection at home only led the 1st Earl to a more deeply entrenched belief in the existing social hierarchy, and to a determination to resist reform. After an inspection of Lincoln Castle Gaol in his role as Lord-lieutenant of Lincolnshire, he is said to have described what was one of the bleakest establishments of its time as far too much 'like a palace'. And in 1831, when the Lords threw out the Reform Bill that sought to widen the franchise, he set to to defend Belton against possible attack by rioters. A household militia was sworn in, drilled and put on watch, but the attack never came.

Autocratic and authoritarian, the 1st Earl was also an erudite and cultured man. He supported the excavation of Roman remains in the vicinity of Belton park – an act which caused J. P. Neale, in his *Views of Seats* (1819), to describe him as 'an accomplished and polite scholar'. His taste for the antique led him to tour Italy with the classical scholar John Chetwode Eustace in 1802, and to correspond with the antiquary Edward Dodwell, whose *Classical and Topographical Tour through Greece* appeared in 1819. He was also a patron of contemporary artists, including Antonio Canova and Sir Richard Westmacott. Following the death in 1814 of his first wife Sophia Hume, and after advice from Westmacott, he commissioned Canova to produce the enormous statue of Religion which forms the centrepiece of her memorial in Belton church. In 1826 Westmacott designed the monument to the 1st Earl's second wife, Caroline.

Sir Jeffry Wyatville

Like his father before him, the 1st Earl was swift to introduce new changes to Belton, and, again like his father, he chose a Wyatt as his architect. Jeffry Wyatt (1766–1840), the nephew of James, is perhaps best known today for his drastic remodelling of Windsor Castle in Berkshire (1824–40), which earned him a knighthood, the motto 'Windsor', and a change of name to Wyatville. But already in 1809, when Brownlow commissioned the first in a series of alterations to the house and grounds at Belton, Jeffry had built up a successful country house practice, providing mainly Tudor-Gothic and Elizabethan designs for an aristocratic clientele.

Wyatville's work at Belton, which covers the years 1809–20, included the creation of the present Orangery (designed in 1811, but not

John, 1st Earl Brownlow, who commissioned Sir Jeffry Wyatville to redecorate the Red Drawing Room

*(Above) The Red Drawing Room in the 1850s;
a watercolour by Amelia Cust*

put up until *c.*1819), the Lion Exedra (1820), and a brewhouse on the south side of the stable courtyard. Internally, his major work was to convert the upper part of the old kitchen in the north-west wing into a new room to house the Brownlows' growing collection of books. The kitchens were re-sited in a wing on the west side of the house. Jeffry's scheme for the decoration of the new 'great library' and its adjoining ante-library was drawn up between July 1809 and 1810.

The new libraries were furnished in 1811 by Gillow & Co., which supplied chairs, window curtains, 'a handsome writing Table with leather top inlaid with metal', and '34 Green silk Curtains for the Book case Doors'. New double doors opened out of the ante-library into the Red Drawing Room, which Wyatville had heavily gilded by George Hutchinson, the

painter employed for most of the work at Belton. Gillows again provided much of the furniture, as well as hanging the crimson damask which covered the walls. The doors to the Marble Hall and Saloon were regrained; Wyatville designed a new geometrically patterned plasterwork ceiling for the Saloon – the old one was in poor condition; and he altered the main staircase, providing it with a 'Vitruvian Scroll for the String of the best Stairs', graining on the wainscot and its predominantly white and gold colour scheme, which was renewed in 1963 and 2001.

Wyatville's alterations were completed by the mid-1820s, but during the decade which followed, the 1st Earl contemplated further changes to Belton, consulting Sir Robert Smirke, who drew up a plan for a new office wing. In 1821 Anthony Salvin designed and built a boathouse in the park, and a village cross, pub, blacksmith's house and cottages in Belton village, mostly in a Tudor style.

Serving a queen

The 1st Earl's third wife, Emma Sophia Edgcumbe, was the daughter of the 2nd Earl of Mount Edgcumbe (of Cotehele, in Cornwall) and Lady Sophia Hobart (of Blickling, in Norfolk – both also properties of the National Trust). Having spent her youth trailing round Europe with her uncle, Lord Castlereagh, on his official visits as Foreign Secretary, Emma Sophia was married to the 1st Earl in July 1828, and two years later was made Lady-in-Waiting to Queen Adelaide, wife of William IV. A close relationship developed between the two, and in September 1841, when the widowed Adelaide had embarked on her wanderings following the accession of Queen Victoria in 1837, she came to stay at Belton, bringing with her the Duchess of Gloucester. Young Sir John Brownlow's best bedchamber on the first floor in the centre of the north front was redecorated for the occasion, and was duly renamed the Queen's Bedroom.

The Egerton legacy

The 1st Earl's eldest son, John, Viscount Alford (1812–51), died before his father, but while he never inherited Belton, he was indirectly responsible for a dramatic rise in the fortunes of the Brownlow family. His mother Sophia – the wife commemorated by Canova's statue – was one of only two daughters of Lady Amelia Hume, the sister and heiress of the unmarried 8th and last Earl of Bridgewater. As Lady Farnborough, Sophia's sister, was childless, Alford became Bridgewater's nearest male relative, and in 1849 he inherited the vast Egerton estates, worth

some £70,000 a year. These included Ashridge Park in Hertfordshire, the creation of two architects with whom the Brownlows were already familiar; it was begun in 1808 by James Wyatt, and completed after his death in 1813 by Wyatville.

The prospect of owning Ashridge – a vast and sprawling Gothic fantasy in the grand manner – must have appealed to the young Viscount, whose tastes ran to the medieval, as did those of so many Tory romantics reared on a diet of *Ivanhoe* and *Kenilworth*.

The Egerton legacy came with a rather curious condition: to keep his inheritance, Viscount Alford had to obtain the lapsed dukedom or marquessate of Bridgewater within five years. In the event, he had little opportunity to do so, dying in 1851 at the early age of 38. But other claimants contested the will, and at

(Right) Emma Sophia, Countess Brownlow, who was lady-in-waiting to Queen Adelaide

the first hearing of the case in the same year a decision was given against the Brownlow family, only to be reversed after an appeal to the House of Lords in 1853.

The 1st Earl Brownlow died in 1853, two years after his son. The family estates passed to his eleven-year-old grandson, John William Spencer Egerton Cust (1842–67), whose mother, Lady Marian, became chatelaine of both Belton and Ashridge during the boy's minority. The daughter of the 2nd Marquess of Northampton, Lady Marian was a talented artist. She pioneered the academic study of needle-work, helping to found the Royal School of (Art) Needlework in 1872, and writing an influential work on *Needlework as Art*. Her London home in Kensington Gore became a centre for gatherings of artistic and literary figures.

(Left) Lady Marian Alford, who was a talented needle-woman

Mud and medievalism

Alford was one of the thirteen knights-in-armour who paid homage to the Queen of Love and Beauty before entering the lists at the famous – and rain-sodden – tournament at Eglinton Castle in Ayrshire in August 1839. He was also instrumental in providing the crowds gathered to watch the jousting with the only moment of excitement in an otherwise disastrous affair. In the final 'grand equestrian mêlée' with broadswords, the Marquess of Waterford hit him on the head, and both opponents lost their tempers and started whacking each other in earnest.

The Knight Marshal had to step in and separate them. The event is recorded in John Richardson's illustrated volume, *The Eglinton Tournament* (1843), which is kept in the Library at Belton.

Adelbert, 3rd Earl Brownlow, who presided over Belton in its High Victorian heyday

Adelbert, 3rd Earl Brownlow
Returning to Caroline Belton

The 2nd Earl Brownlow died unmarried in 1867 aged only 25, having had little time to make his mark on Belton. This task was left to his brother Adelbert, the charismatic 3rd and last Earl (1844–1921). 'Addy' was by all accounts an extremely good-looking young man, tall and handsome, with delightfully unaffected, almost boyish manners, and full of stories about the adventures which he had had while serving abroad in the army. His wife Adelaide, whom he married in 1868, was a match for him in looks. The daughter of the 18th Earl of Shrewsbury, she and her two sisters were described in 1893 as 'the salt of the earth … they looked like the Three Fates'.

It was the 3rd Earl and Lady Adelaide who were responsible for what is perhaps the most remarkable of all the changes which Belton has undergone since Young Sir John's time.

Although they lived for much of the year either at Ashridge or at their London town house in Carlton House Terrace, during the last three decades of the 19th century they devoted a great deal of time and money to remodelling the Lincolnshire house.

The 3rd Earl's architect – whose identity remains a mystery – systematically replaced those Caroline features which had been stripped away a century before by James Wyatt. The balustrade had already been restored to the roof some years earlier, and now the cupola was reinstated, and the dormers were given back their pediments. A domestic wing on the north side of the West Court was also added, linking the house with the stableyard; and several of the interiors were redecorated.

The Brownlows decided on designs provided by the firm of George Jackson & Sons of Rathbone Place in London, which carried out much of the restoration work at Belton. Jacksons produced a splendid Edward Goudge pastiche with garlands of fruit and flowers, incorporating the arms of the 3rd Earl, for the Saloon ceiling; and an equally impressive piece of neo-Caroline plasterwork for Wyatville's small dining room on the south front. This became known as the Tapestry Room, after Addy and Adelaide unearthed Viscount Tyrconnel's Diogenes tapestries – they were being used as carpets in the attics – and installed them there. At the same time Brownlow put up new panelling in this room, some of which came from an oak which was

The Souls

Lord and Lady Brownlow were on the fringes of the Souls, that élite group of high-minded, idealistic and intellectual aristocrats, whose inner band included George Curzon, Arthur Balfour, Margot Tennant and Harry Cust. The group is said to have been named at a dinner party given by the Brownlows in 1888, when Lord Charles Beresford mocked their intensity: 'You all sit and talk about each other's souls – I shall call you the Souls.'

struck by lightning in 1875 at Brandon, a few miles north of Belton.

Elsewhere in the house, Addy and Adelaide redecorated the Boudoir on the first floor, retaining Wyatt's cornice frieze and ceiling, and covering the walls with a green striped silk damask. They also began to transform Wyatville's library into a new 'French Dining Room' (although its 'French' character evidently did not last long, since in 1880 Morris & Co provided it with a 'new stained oak dining table'). The Hondecoeter Room, as it became known, takes its name from the huge canvases of garden scenes by the 17th-century Dutch artist Melchior d'Hondecoeter, which the 3rd Earl acquired in 1873.

The conversion of the library into a dining room meant that a new place had to be found for the Brownlow books. During his brief tenure as the 2nd Earl Brownlow, Addy's brother had consulted yet another member of the Wyatt clan, Matthew Digby Wyatt, about the possibility of turning James Wyatt's great drawing room into a library, and the 3rd Earl decided to continue with the plan, employing the local Grantham firm of John Hall to fit out the new room with the bookcases which Wyatville had designed for the old library 60 years before.

Addy and Adelaide Brownlow did more than any previous generation of Brownlows to restore and maintain the original character of Young Sir John's house. More than this, the neo-Caroline interiors which they commissioned have become important historical landmarks in themselves, as the forerunners of a new attitude towards the architecture of the late 17th century. But however important

to posterity, their renovation of Belton was only a small part of the Brownlows' lives. Addy entered national politics, holding minor office in three Conservative administrations, as Parliamentary Secretary to the Local Government Board (1885–6), Paymaster General (1887–9), and Under-Secretary of State for War (1889–92). With Adelaide, he also played his part in county society to the hilt, whether it was as Lord-lieutenant of Lincolnshire, Colonel of the local militia, attending the annual Hospital Ball in Grantham, or entertaining neighbours at Belton.

(Right) Adelaide, Countess Brownlow; painted by Frederick Leighton in 1879 (Staircase Hall). Mary Gladstone was enchanted by this dress: 'At teatime today in white embroidered with gold regular toga sort of thing … Oh lovely!'

The 20th century

Harry Cust

Lord Brownlow's heir was his cousin, Harry Cust (1861–1917). The high-minded idealism of the Souls was tempered, in Cust's case at least, by a penchant for fast living. When Evan Charteris, a founder-member of the Souls, was a struggling young barrister, he once invited Harry to dinner, together with an eminent solicitor whom he was trying to impress. Cust drank rather too much, and the next day Charteris sent him a telegram saying, 'You have ruined my life but it was worth it.' Harry replied with another: 'That is a sentiment I am more used to hearing from women.'

Cust was a notorious and compulsive womaniser. Ettie Grenfell, later Lady Desborough, was one of his many admirers, much to the chagrin of her son Julian, who in spite of a grudging respect for Cust's intellectual abilities, described him as 'an old bore with vulgar hair and disgusting habits'. After a torrid affair with Violet, wife of the future 8th Duke of Rutland, in 1893 he married Nina, the daughter of Sir William Welby-Gregory, whose Denton estate lay between Belton and the Rutlands' domain in the Vale of Belvoir. Unfortunately for Nina, marriage had little effect on his lifestyle, and Lord and Lady Brownlow took pity on her, often inviting her to stay with them at Belton.

A marble bust of Harry Cust by his wife Nina

Loose living apart, Harry Cust was extremely bright, and from an early age he was expected to do great things. A Unionist MP for Lincolnshire (1890–5) and for Bermondsey (1900–6), he was a significant figure on the London literary scene, exercising a great deal of influence as editor of the *Pall Mall Gazette* in the 1890s, and emerging as a poet of some distinction. His best-known work, 'Non Nobis' ('Not unto us the rapture of the day, The peace of night, or love's divine surprise'), appeared in the *Oxford Book of English Verse*. But his political and literary pursuits were to some extent merely ways of passing the time while he waited to inherit Belton and Ashridge from his childless cousin.

That was never to be. The 3rd Earl outlived him by four years, and in January 1921 the barony and all the estates passed not to the 'old bore with … disgusting habits', but to his younger brother, Adelbert Salusbury Cockayne Cust (1867–1927). In 1917 Harry was buried in Belton church, where he is commemorated by a life-sized effigy – carved by the patient and devoted Nina. In 1955, 38 years after her husband's death, she was laid to rest beside him.

Adelbert, 5th Lord Brownlow
Cutting back

The heir to Belton (although not to the Earldom, which became extinct) succeeded only after some delay. He and his family were holidaying quietly in a *pension* in the South of France, and for some days nobody, not even the British Consul, could find them to inform them of the last Earl's death. Having lived on army pay for most of their lives, the 5th Baron Brownlow and his wife Maud were unused to the style of life which the Brownlow inheritance seemed to promise. (They did, however, splash out on a taxi to take them from Cannes to Menton when the news finally reached them.) However, that inheritance was not as lavish as it might have seemed. Land values and rentals were falling; Belton was mortgaged; and the duties that had to be paid on the death of the 3rd Earl meant that Ashridge, its collection of pictures, and some of its furnishings had to be sold off. The Hertfordshire estates were given over to trustees to deal with, and the new Lady Brownlow had the poignant task of choosing which furniture, china, glass and linen should go to Belton – and which should stay. Over the next six years, enormous cuts in staff and other savings in running costs meant that Brownlow was able to pay off the mortgage and still set aside £60,000 towards his own death duties.

Perry Brownlow and the Abdication Crisis

His son, Peregrine Adelbert Cust (1899–1978), who inherited Belton in 1927, was destined to play a part in British history which had repercussions far beyond the walls of Belton. He is best known today, not for the country house which he so carefully preserved, but for his role in the Abdication Crisis of 1936.

During the early 1930s Perry Brownlow and his first wife Kitty were important members of the 'Fort Circle', often staying at Fort Belvedere, the private residence in Windsor Great Park of Edward, Prince of Wales. In his turn, the Prince occasionally came to stay at Belton, as did Wallis Simpson. When Edward succeeded to the throne in January 1936, Lord Brownlow was appointed Lord-in-Waiting to the King, and throughout that year he was his closest friend and one of his most valued advisers. It was to him that the King's supporters turned when news of Edward's intention to marry Mrs Simpson began to spread, seeking to persuade him to bring pressure on the American divorcee to give up the King and leave the country. But Brownlow feared that if Mrs Simpson did leave England, Edward would soon follow her, precipitating the forced abdication which everybody sought to avoid. So he tried, against the King's wishes, to persuade Mrs Simpson to come to Belton instead. From there she would at least be on hand to provide Edward with advice and moral support – and she might perhaps be able to prevent him from doing anything hasty.

Perry Brownlow, who played a key role in the Abdication Crisis of 1935

On 3 December 1936 the crisis was aired in the British press for the first time. Backed into a corner, Stanley Baldwin announced the next day that the Government could not approve Edward's plan to marry Mrs Simpson without making her Queen, and to resign all claims to the throne on behalf of any children they might have. The King left London for Fort Belvedere, and Perry Brownlow and Wallis Simpson went, not to Belton, but to Cannes, where they stayed until the crisis was over.

It quickly became clear that Edward could not keep both his throne and the woman he loved. In Cannes Perry Brownlow pressured Mrs Simpson to renounce the King; and on 7 December it was decided that she should issue a statement saying that she was prepared to give him up: Perry advised her on its wording, and read it to waiting reporters. But the final choice lay with Edward; and on 10 December Baldwin entered the House of Commons and read the royal message of abdication.

The gift to the National Trust

During the decades which followed, Belton remained much as the 6th Lord Brownlow had found it. However, by the 1960s it had become clear that the old house was in urgent need of repair. So, between 1961 and 1964, he commissioned the architect Francis Johnson to carry out a major restoration programme, with grant-aid from the Historic Buildings Council. The roof was re-slated and the leading was replaced, and Johnson struggled to cure a serious outbreak of dry rot, which had been aggravated by a series of burst pipes during the bad winter of 1929. Panelling was taken down and repaired in many of the rooms, notably the Staircase Hall and the Chapel; cornices were cut and replaced; and a number of rooms were redecorated.

The 6th Lord Brownlow died in 1978. Six years later his son Edward gave Belton House, its garden, a quantity of garden sculpture and much of the contents to the National Trust. In addition to this, the Trust bought the park of 1,317 acres and more of the contents of the house, and established an endowment fund to maintain the property. The total cost of £8 million was almost wholly met by the National Heritage Memorial Fund. The Belmount Tower, built for Viscount Tyrconnel in 1749–51, together with land leading up to the skyline and an important part of the village, was subsequently acquired with money bequeathed by Mr A. Oliver, with further assistance from the NHMF.

In May 1984 Lord Brownlow held a sale of those contents which would not be acquired by the Trust. Many of these furnishings and pictures had come to Belton since the 19th century. The principal family collections, the portraits, the porcelain, much of the silver, the complete library and the outstanding items of furniture remain at Belton, in the care of the National Trust.

The National Trust

Since the National Trust acquired Belton in 1984, it has done much to protect, conserve and redisplay the house's treasures, with an unobstrusive fire detection system and a new silver museum, among many other things. Year by year, the principal rooms have been revived, and new ones added to the tour. Recent work has transformed the Queen's Bedroom, the Red Drawing Room and the Blue Bedroom. There is always something new to enjoy.

(Right) The huge decorative paintings by Melchior d'Hondecoeter were restored in the late 1980s as part of the National Trust's care for Belton's collections